American Women: The Changing Image

AMERICAN WOMEN:

The Changing Image

Edited by Beverly Benner Cassara

Contributors

Ethel J. Alpenfels   Dorothy Hopper

Pearl S. Buck   Edith F. Hunter

Agnes De Mille   Vivian C. Mason

Lillian M. Gilbreth   Margaret Mead

Bessie Hillman   Agnes E. Meyer

Chase Going Woodhouse

Beacon Press   Boston

Library of Congress catalog card number: 62-13636
Printed in the United States of America

Fifth printing, October 1968

FOREWORD

Whether the idea appeals to all women or not, the status of women in our society is changing significantly. However, the ambiguity which clouds the whole problem of woman's role in the modern age leaves some women denying the existence of change itself, while others suffer because avenues of self-expression and individual development supposedly open to them are still inaccessible.

Few women are untouched by this dilemma. The forces of social change are making new standards for women. Can women direct this change to the best interests of themselves, of men and of society in general?

This book has been published because the Alliance of Unitarian Women believes that women should face the problem and come to grips with it. Men as well as women should read this book, since its concerns are properly the concerns of both sexes.

I wish to extend grateful acknowledgment to the many friends whose wise and generous counsel has made this book possible. Among these are Doris Holmes, whose concern about the role of modern woman sparked the idea of such a book, and the assistant editor, Constance H. Burgess, whose loyal support of the project contributed to many creative solutions of problems. Valuable advice on specific problems was contributed by Roy Wilkins, Walter Reuther, Laura Hersey, Esther Sweet, David Riesman, Lewis Dexter, Carol Morris, Max Awner and Ernest Cassara. Jean Tillinghast handled many technical matters with great efficiency. Very special thanks go to Laura Devlin and others of the Beacon Press staff.

BEVERLY BENNER CASSARA

CONTENTS

CONTENTS

INTRODUCTION

Margaret Mead

Margaret Mead, Associate Curator of Ethnology at the American Museum of Natural History and Adjunct Professor of Anthropology at Columbia University, received her B.A. from Barnard College and her M.A. and Ph.D. from Columbia University. An internationally known anthropologist, Dr. Mead is author of many books and articles including *Coming of Age in Samoa* and *New Lives for Old: A Cultural Transformation—Manus, 1928-1953.*

During the last fifty years we have been preoccupied with those changes in women's role which are giving women increasing freedom to enter professions outside the home and increasing freedom from drudgery within the home. But a number of other changes are taking place, concurrently and little recognized, which may have profound effects upon the way in which women's feminine nature and capabilities contribute to the welfare of mankind. In a period of history when it is of the greatest importance that we mobilize all possible efforts to "cherish and protect the lives of men and the life of the world," it may be well to ask: What has happened to those roles which have historically belonged to women—to care for the young, nurse the sick, lay out the dead, attend women in childbirth, comfort the sorrowful, quiet unruliness and temper hotheadedness with gentleness and wisdom, and in many instances elect a life of single blessedness devoted to God or God's children? A mere recitation of these historical roles sounds strange and old-fashioned; the very vocabulary is out of date.

We may think of the family as having begun, in our far prehistoric past, when males extended their protection over specific females and their offspring, during a longer and longer childhood, and established the habit of hunting, not for themselves alone but for a mate waiting to prepare for the little group who lived together. This change in behavior probably roughly coincided with the loss of a specific breeding season. Females became receptive to male advances all the year round, and family life—based on regular sex relations on the one hand, and the provision and preparation of food on the other—in which a male and one or more females cared for the young, was established. In all probability such primitive families existed before any greater division of labor or elaboration of social organization or religious belief had been developed. Such families, however, needed group life for safety, mutual support and to provide mates from outside the household, so that intrafamilial strife between fathers and growing sons over the possession of the sisters could be prevented.

It took hundreds of thousands of years to develop the very simple cultures that we find in remote parts of the world, and longer still to develop the great civilizations to which our own modern civilization is heir. Through the ages, the central pattern of the family and the division of labor between the sexes survived; men went out from the hearth for food, to protect and to conquer, to explore and to organize. Women stayed near the hearth, cared for the young children and prepared the food. However much later generations elaborated this pattern, with greatly extended families, complex systems of feudal interrelationships, and one-sex religious communities, this central core remained. But much was added to it. To the care of the infant and toddler was added the protection of young people through adolescence, the care of the sick and the care of the old. And a place was found for the wisdom and wider generosity of women past childbearing, who were heavy with the memories of earlier solutions and free to care, not only for their own children— with fierce maternal protectiveness, as the young mothers did—but with a wider concern for all the children within the community. Elaborate rituals grew up around death, and it was women who straightened the limbs of the dead and washed their bodies for burial. Knowledge of midwifery grew, and it was women who attended women in labor, washed the newborn, and wrapped him, in bark or swaddling clothes, and laid him on his first bed.

When the Judaic-Christian tradition flowered in a new concern for the welfare of the poor and the sick and the orphaned, it was women who arranged to take on these widened responsibilities. First as "widow," then as deaconesses, then—organized in a way that made them more amenable to male authority—as nuns, they continued these extended activities that had once been confined to the home. Then as nurses, and as teachers, their traditional role was widened. In the early days of the United States, it was the raised voices of valiant older women, who fought against slavery, against child labor, against the horrors of the slums; who fought for schools, for libraries, playgrounds, legislation and funds, to improve our communities and to protect our children. Many of these women were unmarried, and gave, as Jane Addams did, their entire lives to make a world safe, not for their own children, but for all children. In England, even as late as World War II, it was the devoted unmarried woman who carried a tremendous amount of the burden in the days of bombing and buzz bombs.

We are the inheritors of this tradition: of women who left their homes—many of them never to return—to extend the services once performed within the home to the wider world outside. We may well ask, in these days of great freedom, when education is as open to women as men, when the great professions of medicine and law, teaching and scientific research are open to women, how do we stand?

The answer is very simple; we stand very badly indeed. If we look first at the ancient occupations like bathing the dead—this is now in the hands of morticians, a male profession conducted for profit. Midwifery, and the loving induction of mother and infant into a satisfactory symbiotic relationship is now in the hands of male obstetricians, followed by male pediatricians. Visiting the widowed and the sorrowful is done by male insurance agents—again as part of the profit organization of society. Dedicating one's life to God or human welfare is becoming steadily more unpopular; the teaching and nursing orders depend upon bringing in women from the less sophisticated parts of the world. Bedside nursing is repudiated by the trained nurse as beneath her high level of education. The care of the infirm old has been put as far outside the home as possible and delegated to institutions in which gadgets replace tenderness and the television set the friendly personal voice. Meanwhile some 500,000 surplus older women, many of them with more than adequate means are not extending their activities on behalf of mankind, but shrinking them to the preservation of their own private, and often boring existences. Neither their fortunes, nor their hearts nor their imaginations are placed at the service of the wider world. Finally, in such matters as peace and bread, measures to protect the world from war, and to provide food for the children who suffer and die from preventable malnutrition—are women in the forefront of organized movements of this sort today?

On the whole it is not a very pretty picture, and we may well ask why. Why have we returned, for all our great advances in technology, to the Stone Age arrangement in which women's main ambition is to acquire and hold a mate, to produce or adopt children who are to be the exclusive delight and concern of a single married pair, and in which work outside the home, whether it be such traditional occupations as teaching or nursing, or office or technical work holds no attraction in itself, unless it is subservient to the demands of an individual household, albeit a household equipped with enough hardware to bring water and health to villages of a hundred people; a household from which hundreds of pounds of waste materials from unnecessary packaging are extruded; a household carefully protected against the dangers and contaminations of broken homes—even homes broken by death.

Woman has returned, each to her separate cave, waiting anxiously for her separate mate and children to return, guarding her mate jealously against other women, almost totally unaware of any life outside her door. The woman who does not marry is frowned upon and discriminated against, given neither status nor honor. Religious dedication is now called by various psychiatric names, and the dedicated are suspected of neuroses. Interest in any kind of work which might take precedence over the desire to have a family is discouraged; girls are admonished to study typing rather than mathematics, and if, after the children are grown, women look for some greater meaning in life, their eyes are turned towards a hobby, self-fulfillment, seldom towards activities on behalf of the larger community. Community busywork—Scouts, PTA, local Community Chest drives—have become part of the homemaking activities of the mothers of young children, as they attempt to make their community good for their children, and well protected against those whose children might need help, and who would therefore lower the status of the little green islands on which their own children are safe.

In this retreat into fecundity—the United States has the fastest growing population in the world today—it is not the individual young girl, or young wife or older woman who is to blame; it is the climate of opinion that has developed in this country, to which its leaders have succumbed, and which now is stifling the ethical life of the nation. To alter the trend, it will be necessary to make some very basic changes in the present attitudes of both men and women, but it is enough of a project to start with women themselves, and especially with women who are rearing daughters, guiding girls or preparing to be complacent grandmothers.

We might start with some very basic questions: Are women to be seen as individuals with special capabilities and possibilities, or primarily as wives and mothers? Are we to continue to provide an education for girls that is comparable to an education for boys and then reward with praise and approval the girl who makes no use of her education, and ignore the one who does? Are we to do nothing about the difficulty girls encounter getting a medical education because they are expected to, and do, give up practicing when they marry? Are we going to accept the popular present-day thesis that every adult who isn't conspicuously occupied with married life every minute, from puberty until the imbalance between the sexes condemns some women to widowhood, has something wrong with him, at the best neurosis, at the worst character disorders and perversions that may even lead to crime and treason? Are we going to continue and exacerbate the practice of forcing immature girls, and even more immature boys, into a travesty of courtship, hustling them towards marriage before they are in any way ready for it? Are we going to perpetuate the present distrust of the genuineness of any woman who wishes to devote herself to work, whether it be art or science, medicine or the religious life? Are we going to condone the present treatment of the older woman who wants to do useful work, both by Social Security regulations and present employment practices? Are we going to do nothing about the plight of the single woman who must live overseas, or in a strange city, all alone because she has neither salary nor living allowance which would permit her to bring her dependent relatives—a mother, a sister, a niece—to live with her? Are we going to ask nothing of widows with incomes except that they stay well, keep themselves amused and don't make demands on their married children?

It is against this kind of background and this order of problems that we can consider the role of women in the emerging world of the future in which we will depend more and more upon science. One reason that women played such an insignificant role in science is that science has, in many ways, been alienated from human life, departmentalized and provincial. The human sciences are the sciences in which women have been most welcomed and in which they have done the best work. But the great majority of natural scientists have been either indifferent or contemptuous of the human sciences. Science fiction, which has done so much to prepare boys for under-

standing and participating in scientific activity, is almost all written
in profound ignorance of human beings, as either the poet, the
novelist or the social scientist knows them. So girls are repelled by
science fiction, and the gap in scientific understanding between boys
and girls widens, in spite of higher and higher general education for
girls as well as for boys.

Yet, if we are to have a world in which human beings can live,
it is more scientific activity that we need, not less. Women must
take their places in a world about which we are learning more and
more. And there are two courses open to them, to take alternatively,
sequentially or both together: to become the teacher-mothers of infant scientists, or to engage in immediate scientific activities, as
teachers, researchers, planners, engineers, therapists. There is abun-
dant evidence that the very early education of the child, long before
school begins, can lay the groundwork for thinking. A mother who
knows nothing about science is a mother whose child is that much
handicapped. A mother who dislikes the idea of space because it
might take her husband or children too far is bringing up members
of a generation of stay-at-homes who will prefer mowing lawns with
a power lawnmower to venturing towards the stars, in theory or in
actuality.

And as long as women, in desperate cave-women style, devote
their whole lives to narrow domesticity, first in schoolgirl dreaming
and searching for roles which make them appealingly ignorant, then
as mothers and then as grandmothers, our scientific activity will
remain one-sided, with an overemphasis on power, and an under-
emphasis on human values.

Long ago, when men huddled together in small groups, in caves,
straw huts or platforms in trees, the fact that there were a few old
women past childbearing was a great strength to a group. The old
women remembered what had been done in the past. The old
women, now grouped with the old men whose numbers had been
decimated by the precariousness of hunting and warfare, could take
responsibility for the whole group, could lead them in time of
famine to where food had been found in a previous emergency.
They could draw on a lifetime of experience: in childbirth, in re-
calling to life those who fainted, in staunching the blood of the
wounded.

Today our millions of lives are in even greater danger than when
human beings clustered for safety around a fire which no one knew
how to make and which must not be allowed to go out. Now, as

then, we need those who can take a wider responsibility, some women who are not burdened by infants in their arms, some who can think for the whole, work for the whole. For we have need of a new invention, some way in which we can take responsibility for the whole of mankind, while recognizing that the *governments* of some nations are inimical to ours, and so to us. Perhaps we have so few crusaders now because so many of the battles fought by crusading women of the past appear to be won. But this is dangerous ethnocentric complacency. The intrinsic cherishing role of women for children—not just her own, but all children—is needed now as never before. For now we cannot even protect our own children unless we find a way of protecting the children of the enemy also. Or there will be no children to cherish.

I. The Challenge to Modern Women

CHANGING RELATIONSHIPS BETWEEN MEN AND WOMEN

Pearl S. Buck

Pearl S. Buck is the eminent and prolific American novelist and author. The daughter of missionaries, she was born in West Virginia and brought up in China where she also spent much of her adult life. Her B.A. is from Randolph-Macon Women's College and her M.A. is from Cornell; Pearl Buck has also received countless honorary degrees. With one child of her own, Mrs. Walsh has adopted eight children, two of them of part Asian ancestry, two of part Negro ancestry. She is a former member of three university faculties in China, and she has promoted the adoption of many Asian children in this country through the agency she founded, Welcome House. Mrs. Walsh received the Pulitzer Prize in 1932 for her novel, *The Good Earth*, and the Nobel Prize for Literature in 1938.

Twenty-five years ago, when I first came to the United States, my own country, to live and to make my permanent home, I was deeply interested in the American woman. My experience and training had acquainted me with the Asian woman, but I had known few Western women and none intimately. The American woman was new and exciting. She had a freedom to which I was not accustomed. She could come and go as she liked in city and country, even alone. She could go to school, to college, to work. At the same time she had an amazing amount of privilege. She need not work outside the home, she was treated with courtesy, and to a degree somewhat shocking to me, she was indulged by father and husband. Because she was a woman she was excused from hard physical labor and little mental effort was expected. She was accustomed to being cared for.

3

The women of Asia are strong and independent. They have not had the advantages or disadvantages of a chivalric tradition. They are not accustomed to being cared for. Their place in society was, and is, defined but powerful.

In the family the woman was the *de facto* ruler, although she was trained to defer outwardly to her father, her husband or her older brother. Men exercised their authority within the accepted limits and did not interfere with women in the home. When modern times provided the vote, women received it at the same time men did. In fact, Chinese women had the vote before American women did. Whatever deprivation, illiteracy and lack of opportunity Chinese women suffered men suffered, too.

True, woman's place was in the home, but then the seat of power in Chinese society was the home. Unspoiled and without special privilege, Asian women did the practical work of life. She worked in the fields beside her husband and she stood behind the counter if he kept a shop. Men took it for granted that women worked wherever there was work to be done. Under the Communists, woman is expected to take her full place as a citizen, and now the goal is to release her from the home. It is considered reprehensible that a woman should cook for one family, or devote herself to the children of one family. If she wants to be a housewife she should be cooking and caring for the children of many. Under communism men insist that women take full part in the industrial and cultural life of the nation, and they use ruthless means to accomplish the fact.

In the United States, I found a paradox. The American woman enjoyed opportunity equal with men for education and training in the professions, but she did not utilize this education and training. Instead she married and went into a house and devoted herself to a small group, her own family. I hasten to say that I am all for marriage and home and children. Nor do I minimize the important role of women as wife and mother. The question, however, was whether the woman was sufficiently or

properly trained even for this position, if it were to be her only
one or, at best, her chief role. To educate her for mobility and
freedom and then deny her that same mobility and freedom can
lead only to frustration, and a frustrated woman is not a good
wife and mother, however much she may love her husband and
children.

I observed frustration in the American woman. She often
denied her frustration, insisting that she wanted to be married,
that nobody had forced marriage on her, that it was woman's
highest calling, her natural place and so forth. Nevertheless,
in spite of such protestations, it was obvious that she was dis-
contented in at least part of her being and most of the time. Her
life was hectic between kitchen and school, her time schedule
not her own but that of husband and children. To serve is beautiful, but only if it is done with joy and a whole heart and a free
mind. The American woman served her family as a duty, bright-
ened by love, it is true, and by intervals of joy, but the atmosphere she created in so doing was not one of continued content.

From early observations I wrote a small book entitled *Of
Men and Women.* This little effort has brought me thousands
of letters from all over the world, from both men and women.
Now, two decades later, I am often asked if I would write the
same book again. My reply is that I would, but I would add a
second part. Much of what was true a quarter of a century ago
is still true. Women's education is the same, but her frustrations
are more obvious even though some small attempt is being made
to alleviate her discontent. She is working outside the home to
the extent of supplying about one-third of the labor force in
the whole country, but her basic situation remains the same—
with one great, notable, astounding difference: *Women have
not changed, but men have changed.*

Two decades ago the attitude of American men toward
women was tolerant but superior. It was still considered a handicap to a man, a proof of his incompetence if his wife worked.
A man should be able to support his family. This is no longer

true. A young man nowadays expects his wife to help support the family if necessary. If it is not necessary, he encourages her to work at something that may interest her. This can only mean one thing—men have a new estimate of what women can be and should be, and—here is the newness of it—in relation to themselves as men.

This change, which has only been felt since the end of the war, is the result of several forces. Much is being said about the emphasis on sex so apparent in our literature, advertising and social customs. Perhaps this is only the far swing of the pendulum from a past when women were supposed to have little if any interest in sex—a "nice" woman, that is. "Bad" women existed, of course, but for men alone. The daring notion that women enjoy sex as much as men do, if not always in the same way, and the man's discovery that he himself enjoys sex more when she does, has revolutionized the relationship between men and women. They have become partners not only in reproduction but in the joy of creation. Young husbands nowadays want to share more than the moment of conception. They share to a heartening degree the period of pregnancy, the hour of birth, the care of the infant, the growth of the child. Fathers are emerging from their unimportant and sometimes even ludicrous positions to a place of equality with their wives in this most delightful and eminently important function of producing the next generation. I do not say that all men so share, but the younger ones do share and want to share. That is important— they want to share. A real man, moreover, does not feel it threatens his masculinity to change a baby's diapers or to wash the dishes of an evening. It is only the man on the fringe of masculinity who fears that "woman's work" threatens his sex.

The new interest in women which American men are now beginning to evince, may have its roots in a new appreciation of sex as a process, but this appreciation develops into a sensitivity to woman as a human being. He does not now doubt her chastity or think the less of her because she, too, frankly enjoys sex. On the contrary, he is stirred to the depths of his own being, for when once he felt he was alone, he now knows he is not. Since she shares this basic need with him, he is more inclined to share with her the other aspects of his life. He discovers that he likes to talk with her intelligently. He is impatient when her conversation is limited to trivialities and daily humdrum and gossip. Never before has the intelligent and well-educated woman had so much good male companionship as she has now. I am impressed by the fact that while American men are hungry for a fuller companionship with women sexually, they are even more hungry for her intellectual and spiritual companionship.

I wonder how many American women perceive this change in men. If they fail in such recognition, I fear for the world. For man disappointed in woman retreats into a frustration which can compel him to such cynicism and despair that he is capable of brutality, for which indeed she must assume responsibility. If American women can understand the opportunity they now have, and the responsibility, if they can accept both, they will enter upon a new life in which their freedom is as absolute as it can be in a world wracked by huge choices for good or evil. Even so, they may, if they will, if they can grow quickly enough, have a share in deciding what sort of a world it will be. Certainly the decision should not be left to men alone, and it still is as of this moment.

Yes, what I am saying is that nobody is holding women back except women themselves. The challenge that men give us today is simple and clear. They want women to be intelligent as well as beautiful. All the beauty aids in the world will not serve if the brain inside that carefully coiffed—or tousled—head is an empty one, vacuous and small. The instant's diversion will not last. Real men today want real women. Charm must be redefined. It must now include the delight of a mind alive and alert, thinking, imagining, considering, enjoying all that life can offer. Marriage is more than sex, more than home, more than family. For the first time, at least in the United States, I discern in men a yearning desire for women who can fulfill them, and a yearning, equal in its intensity, to fulfill their women. Men are beginning to find new depth in sex, new excitement in love which affects an entire life. Their feeling for women is no longer limited to bed and board.

What a challenge this is to women! How is she responding? Well, as of now, she is frightened. She is the more frightened and even resentful because women of other countries are entering her field. American men are marrying Asian women, European women, wherever they can find the woman they need. The competition grows fierce. So far, American women are responding with panic. They are catching their men very young. I heard a young woman of my acquaintance complain only yesterday that "If you don't get married before you're twenty-two, your chances are slim. Someone else will grab him."

Crude, yes, but it accounts for many of our young marriages. The door of the house is wide open for woman to walk through and into the world, but the stupendous scene beyond terrifies her. She slams the door shut and pulls down the shades. She is so terrified that she sometimes even rails against the exceptional woman, the daring individual who accepts the invitation of the open door and enters into wider opportunity and assumes the new responsibility. Both fear and resentment are natural though not intelligent. Every step toward a new life is terrifying and difficult. A child at birth springs into the larger world beyond the womb not with joy but with loud cries of rage and fright. When death draws near, the dread is deep. What change is this that strips from us the familiar body? We put it off as long as possible.

And let us face it—women have had a good life and an easy one. Yes, yes, I know all about the hardships, the drudgery, the childbearing, the—everything! I maintain that it has been easy. The hardest work in the world is responsibility and men have had it, not women, with notable exceptions. Yes, yes, too, she has had to encourage her man and keep him at it, coax him and feed him food and love and sex in judicious amounts, but he is the one who has shouldered the responsibility and gone out of the open door. And she has stayed safely under the roof, knowing that he would return. Meanwhile she gets the dishes washed, and does the daily chores and keeps busy and within her limits.

The trouble is that the limits must be removed. She must be busy with everything in the world and useful everywhere. If her housewifery prevents her development, then the plain truth is that woman must order her home duties. She must deal more efficiently with housekeeping demands. We would be loath to allow our government to do what the Communists do —tell us sternly that the nation's work can no longer be done by man alone, that woman must help, and if she cannot organize her household work better, government will step in with communal kitchens and day nurseries so that women have nothing to do but work. I hear such rumblings already from men who feel the burden of today's world intolerable upon them, not only the actual labor but the heavier burden of intellectual effort in solving problems and devising new processes. Women's brains are needed today in every field, in the highest echelons. Old prejudices are fading, intelligent men are eagerly seeking intelligence wherever it can be found and they are impatient when intelligent women continue to live in narrow ways, apart from the world's problems and dangers. Now is the time for all good men, *and women.*

The demand is here, the opportunity waits. It is for women now to consider themselves and that open door. There is no household problem which, if women work together, cannot be solved. The question which faces every woman is no longer "Do I want to?" or "How can I?"

The answer is simple. You must! Man needs woman today as never before, if the human race is to be saved. He needs her love and faith, yes, but he needs her actual cooperating work, both of hand and mind, and not only in the home and family. He needs her in every phase and level of national and international life, and, most hopeful of all, he recognizes his need, and is ready to acknowledge it.

> *Let me not to the marriage of true minds,*
> *Admit impediment.*

True marriage is the complete cooperation of men and women in all of life. To such mutual respect and responsibility let women not admit impediment. There are no impediments except in their reluctant minds. I believe that happy families and good children come only from true marriage between man and woman. Similarly and on a universal scale a good society, a safe world, can come only when men and women work together, using their valuable differences and the special contributions of their individual personalities through comradeship and partnership for the human race.

LEADERSHIP RESPONSIBILITIES
OF AMERICAN WOMEN

Agnes E. Meyer

Agnes E. Meyer, author, social worker and humanitarian, has her
B.A. from Barnard College. She has studied at the Sorbonne and at
Columbia University. Mother of five, grandmother of twelve, she has
received many outstanding awards for her service projects for the
betterment of public housing, schooling and medical care. She served
on the White House Conference for Children and Youth and on the
White House Conference on Education. She is the author of several
books including *Journey through Chaos* and *Out of These Roots*.

I feel very strongly that the educated women of America
are not taking their responsibility to the nation's strength and
welfare seriously enough. This is especially true of the present
generation of college students. In former days women went to
college to develop their minds and personalities. Today many
of them frankly go to coeducational institutions of learning to
find a husband as early as possible. This is a frivolous attitude at
a time when our nation is threatened with destruction unless
we develop more highly skilled people and more leadership capable of making enlightened political decisions. It seems tragic
that just when the challenge to women and their opportunities
for service are greatest, the younger ones are so profoundly influenced by the overemphasis on sex now so prevalent in our
whole culture that they are reverting to female rather than to
womanly ideals.

A group of distinguished experts in the medical, social,
political and behavioral sciences has just issued a report in
which they warn, "the United States finds itself today in a world
situation which demands assessment of every resource of physi-

cal, intellectual, and moral power. The role of man in the last half of this century will increasingly be that of an information processor and decision maker. Heavy demands will be placed on human beings at various levels—not only top administration —for correct, closely integrated vital decisions." This report is one of many efforts to waken the American people to the fact that unless we take education more seriously than we have in the past, we shall not long be able to compete with the U.S.S.R. for world leadership.

The interviews with Khrushchev published by Adlai Stevenson, Walter Lippmann and others have made it clear that the Soviets will not resort to war because they now have a firm conviction that they can win their objective—world domination —without it. Thus the cold war has been shifted by the astute leaders of the Kremlin and Peiping from a competition in military power to a competition in brain power. These developments have led Lloyd V. Berkner, of the President's Scientific Advisory Council, to state: "The year 1957 may well stand in history as the point in time at which intellectual achievement forged ahead of weapons and national wealth as instruments of national policy." American women must face the fact that they, their children and their children's children will live, not in a nation that has enjoyed the security denied to all other nations, but in one that will have to demonstrate that democracy can survive even though it no longer enjoys the peaceful isolation which protected our earlier experiments with government.

It is of such importance that women contribute to the productivity of our society that the National Manpower Commission has devoted a whole volume to the subject. While recognizing that women are still torn by the apparent cleavage between work and marriage, the report indicates that this has become a false dichotomy. These tensions are due not to woman's dual role in our technological society, but to the contradiction between outmoded traditions and the urgent need today that educated women function not only as wives and mothers but as creative personalities.

This conflict is largely confined to the educated middle classes; the low income groups feel few such inner tensions because the mother in these families is obliged to help support her children, and her husband accepts the situation for that reason. The problems between husband and wife in our enormous number of well-to-do families would disappear if both realized that our society can no longer afford "the lady of leisure" who, after all, is living at the expense of the working members of society. Before the Industrial Revolution only a small number of aristocratic women lived this artificial life. All other women were economically productive since clothing, food and even commercial products were manufactured in the home by mothers who educated and nursed their children and felt a profound sense of security because their contributions to society meshed closely with those of the father of the family.

The Industrial Revolution temporarily put an end to women's economic role when the factory took over her functions by manufacturing clothing, food and other products more cheaply than she could. Her social value also diminished when children went to public schools, and her humanitarian functions were taken over by professionals.

The wives of factory workers soon followed their husbands' example and became wage earners; but the middle-class woman, the wife of a professional or business man, was left in the home separated from her husband's activities, a home that was empty once the children were grown, with nothing to do except to amuse herself as best she could. It was against this empty life and its economic dependence that the first group of feminists revolted. They were right. For it was and is an artificial situation for women, a by-product of our expanding wealth. Therefore, it is the duty of all married women to realize that our country, hardpressed as it is by a ruthless enemy, can no longer support vast numbers of female drones. And the American man of today should realize that the educated married women who in recent years have achieved positions in the political, business and professional fields, are merely trying to regain the usefulness, status and prestige which every housewife enjoyed in pre-industrial times.

Yet we still have too many able women who are frittering away their lives because they do not realize that any educated mother who does not plan carefully to use her talents when her young children no longer need her, is headed toward futility and unhappiness. For there is nothing more frustrating to a human being than the feeling of native capacities that are withering of atrophy. The fact that we have so many restless, unhappy middle-aged women should be a warning to the girls of today that they must plan their lives as carefully as any young man.

Improved medical care has increased the average life expectancy of women to seventy-two years. Because they marry early and control the size of the family, most women between the ages of thirty-two and thirty-five have already sent their youngest children to school. This means they have forty more years of life to look forward to. Obviously marriage, even if we exclude the possibilities of divorce or the husband's early death, has become only a part-time career for women, demanding their full attention for less than one-third of adult life.

In Alva Myrdal's excellent study of *Women's Two Roles* she says, "The most sensible advice that can be given to young girls under present conditions is that they choose a career best suited to their interests and inclinations and work on the assumption that they will have to live by it, for marriage is not a panacea. They ought, therefore, to be in earnest about their work and under any circumstances even if they get engaged at the training stage, they should try to complete their education so that they can resume their career later on if they want to."

It disturbs me, therefore, to see a definite anti-intellectualism among the present generation of young women. To be sure, anti-intellectualism is a part of the very atmosphere of our country. This was revealed in its crudest form when the late unlamented Senator McCarthy terrorized the country with his brutal arraignment of Communist suspects in the academic world. Women are more deeply affected by the anti-intellectualism which is prevalent in this country than are men. For the anti-rationalism which is reflected in an extreme and unwholesome overemphasis on sex as woman's greatest asset, is undermining her confidence in herself as a balanced personality with definite contributions to make to the realization of democratic ideals.

As one by-product of the economic, social and moral revolution, sex has been debased in our literature, magazines, newspapers, moving pictures, television and advertising. All attempts at censorship are ridiculous when even freely publicized books written by medical men treat the subject of sex as if it were America's favorite indoor sport. The baneful influence of this desecration of the sex instinct is painfully visible. It has resulted in an outbreak of promiscuity even among the very young. In an effort to protect themselves against this, many youngsters resort to the expedient of "going steady" at the noble age of thirteen or fourteen. This not only narrows their lives at a time when they should be enriched by varied human relationships, but leads to marriage at an immature age. That a large percentage of these early marriages end in the divorce courts seems to be no deterrent. The idea is, if you don't succeed at first, try, try again. If a young girl happens to be intelligent, she is made to think that she cannot afford to be a "brain" lest she scare away the men of less intelligence. The answer to that is obvious. Any man who is afraid of a girl's intelligence is not the man for her, since she will be bored to death by him sooner or later, and it is better to find this out before marriage.

Freedom is always a heavy burden in any area of life. But in none is it more fateful a responsibility than in sex relations. Freud has contended again and again that human civilization arose and will always be based on the control and sublimation of the sex instincts by men and women alike. If it were generally understood why this is true, our former negative, puritanical and all too ascetic attitude toward sex would be replaced by a positive and rational—yes—even passionate enthusiasm for high standards of conduct. Young women would realize that nobody suffers more than woman herself if she endangers the home, the stability of society and the progress of civilization when she renounces her rightful position as the guardian of moral values.

As a result of the present overemphasis on the physical aspects of sex, most young girls are no longer interested in developing their minds. The influence begins in high school. Dr. James Conant found that in our better high schools boys with high IQs are taking the important subjects: history, languages, mathematics, physics, chemistry, etc. But the girls with equally high IQs are letting themselves off easily with snap courses in home economics and other forms of distraction. What a waste of potential talent! For even if these girls go to college, they will not be prepared to take full advantage of higher education. They do not seem to realize that in marriage, too, it takes more than cooking and sex appeal to be successful wives and mothers.

And yet I hear too few voices raised among older women against the sex obsession that now pervades our whole culture. It is woman's own fault if she again allows herself to be treated as a female animal. By continually evading educational and professional challenges, women devalue their role in American society. What is the use of college education for women unless it teaches them the importance of a fine discrimination in morals and manners? How can we defend women's right to higher education if they lose their intellectual drive and make no constructive use of their training?

It is unethical, moreover, to accept the benefits of our democratic society without making an adequate return. We must bear in mind that in the college education of women the nation is making a heavy investment. At a time when the competition for a college education is becoming acute, women will be crowded out by men unless they demonstrate that they are making good use of their educational opportunities. There is a growing conviction that college women who are not seriously preparing for a career of some kind should have their right to college education challenged. To be sure, a college education enhances the function of women as wives and mothers, but, as I said before, this is no longer considered a lifetime job. Nor will the corporations give financial grants to the women's colleges unless they produce the kind of workers and executives that society and industry needs. Above all, our women's colleges must produce more intellectual, moral and political leadership for our hard-pressed nation if the graduates are going to do their part in preserving human freedom. What we women must achieve in our country is a transformation of the moral and spiritual climate. We must achieve a new feeling for the tragedy, ambiguity and challenge of being a woman in this age of transition.

This, it seems to me, is the way every educated woman must now visualize her life span: Marriage should be postponed at least until she completes her college course, and preferably two or three years more, in order to get experience in practicing whatever profession she has chosen, or to do graduate work. Overly young marriages should be avoided by any serious young woman. Kipling's line that "a young man married is a young man marred" is equally true for any ambitious young girl. The longer the time the adolescent devotes to the development of the mind, the better for the individual and for the evolution of the race. Also, mature marriages are more apt to be permanent. The American Association of University Women, the League of Women Voters and other women's organizations might well conduct a scientific investigation, gather the pertinent material on the present epidemic of adolescent marriages, and make a veritable campaign to halt this trend. We used to look down on India for encouraging child marriages. Yet our own culture is now encouraging precisely the same questionable behavior.

After marriage every woman must decide carefully how long

her young children will need her concentrated care and attention. But even during this period, if she plans her daily schedule carefully, she should be able to keep in touch with new developments in her profession and be prepared to take it up again as soon as possible. Time is the one thing with which all women should be miserly. In a well-planned daily schedule, given the modern aids to housekeeping, every educated woman can keep up with the problems of the day. To be sure, this is easier in some fields than in others. For example, surgery and other professions that demand constant practice to maintain skills should be avoided; but teaching, research and other scholarly pursuits can be readily adjusted to motherhood and career by any disciplined, intelligent woman. In addition, women's colleges and universities can make arrangements to keep their married graduates in touch with the latest literature on these subjects, and invite them back to the campus for summer courses.

It will take a long time before the woman of average education realizes that she, too, can and must make a contribution to social progress. But if our educated elite set this kind of life pattern, professional women will have a far-reaching influence upon our whole culture. To be sure, they must make a success not only in their chosen field of endeavor but also as wives and mothers. If they fail in either role, it will only damage the status of women in society. But to the extent that they triumph over the difficulties of combining marriage and work, the lives of all women will take on a new significance.

Here is my other appeal: to make the voice of women heard. Women, educated or not, cannot escape their chief responsibility as protectors of the continuity of life. Today every mother should acquire a galvanizing awareness that this continuity is threatened as never before. It is high time for women throughout the world to unite and become more articulate in their demand for the use of scientific research to ease international tensions, for this is the only sound approach to world peace.

We American women must not wait for the government to

tell us what to think and what to do. We must rely on the American genius for voluntary action; we must organize constructive programs in such a way that our government officials will be obliged to respond to our leadership. We women must *act*. For people who look too long upon evil without opposing it go dead inside. They get paralyzed like a chicken looking at a snake. Sometimes I fear that is the way our government officials and our people are reacting to communism. What we need in this country is not more reliance on words and good intentions; what we need is clear thinking and positive actions.

Why should we American women not call another international convention of women, including the Communist women, to be held at The Hague or Geneva? Surely Communist women do not wish their children slaughtered and their cities laid waste any more than we do. Such a conference of women should say to the leaders of whatever country they represent: "You are at present headed toward mass murder and catastrophe. We, as the mothers of the race, emphatically object." If the agenda of such a conference were limited in scope, if we brought to bear on such a conference the whole barrage of social and scientific knowledge we possess today, it could not but be effective. If an international meeting of women made only this one demand for a *continuous* rational approach to peace it would serve notice on our masculine world leadership that the women of all nations reject war as a solution of international conflicts.

Women underestimate their power. Too many of them in the backward countries and even in the Western nations are still caught in a sense of inferiority to the male that has been drummed into them throughout the ages. This timidity has no relevance in a society which has supplanted the advantages of mere physical strength by the importance of intelligence, courage and determination.

II. Women at Home and in the Community

WOMEN AT HOME AND IN THE COMMUNITY

BUT WE MUST CULTIVATE OUR GARDENS

Dorothy Hopper

Dorothy Hopper, mother of two, civic leader, graduate of the University of Washington and former instructor in child development at Simmons College has also been teacher of home economics in public schools. She was the recipient of the 1959 award of the National Conference of Christians and Jews for organizing the Newton, Massachusetts Fair Housing Practices Committee.

A young woman took a teaching position in a remote settlement on the banks of a river which cuts a deep gorge through the Rocky Mountains. She married a local farmer, and moved to an isolated ranch on a sand bar far down the river. She lived there for twenty-five years, connected with civilization only by the river and the railway which clung to its banks.

The nearest farm was miles away; the nearest town several hours by train. The farm was without roads or electricity. The young wife learned to milk cows, drive the team, cut and carry the wood, outwit the temperamental wood stove, keep food without refrigeration, tend the kerosene lamps and cook three heavy meals a day for the rancher and his hired man. Twice a year she took the four children to town for new shoes and a visit to the dentist, and to lay in supplies of flour, salt, sugar, cocoa and a few household supplies. One of the children was lost to the swift river, and the others left home early to board in town for school. She often wondered if she would spend the rest of her life in this lonely spot.

But she had no time to brood. A multitude of small but significant details filled her day, giving her life meaning and purpose. She had the love and respect of her husband, the deep satisfaction of knowing how much he needed her. Her contribution was obvious; she was essential to the life of the farm. In addition to feeling a sense of importance, she relied on a sturdy stoicism which has always been a mainstay of those close to the soil. "We will just have to make the best of it, and be good sports about it," she would say in trying circumstances. Then when the day's work was done, she would sit close to the hissing gasoline lantern and read good books.

I know this woman well, for she was my mother. Her experience demonstrates that happiness in homemaking can be found in what would seem to be the most unfavorable circumstances. In fact, I would maintain that any woman can find being a housewife a rewarding and even exciting experience if she can approach it in a creative way.

In an age of easy formulas, let me offer my own recipe for "The Way," the "Secret of Success." It is of course as simple as common sense and quite as difficult to practice. Let her do these things: first, cultivate the patience of stoicism; second, find satisfaction through service; and third, seize on the possibilities in every situation for new insights, humor and personal growth. Let us consider each of these qualities in turn.

To advocate stoicism may seem incongruous in these times when the cry is to affirm, to assert oneself. Of course we need purposeful choice and action. However, choice involves renunciation of other alternatives and sometimes disappointments. Often there are no alternatives at all, and we rely on plain old grit. We accept the situation and learn to live with it. It is then that a large measure of patience and courage is required.

Patience has never been a particularly American virtue, nor is marriage often thought of in our land as an opportunity for service. Instead, young people are conditioned to think of life as a pursuit of pleasure, and of matrimony as a romantic tonic.

For gay American girls, settling down to homemaking may be one of the major adjustments of life. "School was fun," said one young mother. "I went out a lot, didn't study too hard, and saw my friends between classes and after school. After graduation, I worked in an office, kidded around with the fellows in our section, and had time evenings and weekends for dates and friends. Now I don't see anyone but my husband—on the nights he is home—and the baby keeps me on call twenty-four hours a day. I'm so sick of the same dirty dishes, the same shirts to iron, the same four walls, day after day, and nobody to talk to. I have nice neighbors, but they are busy, too, and besides, aren't interested in the same things I am."

This woman has reached one of the recurrent minor crises in life through which we grow up to maturity. She may continue feeling bored and lonely, or she may face the facts realistically, accept the situation and what it demands of her, and find satisfaction in a creative fulfillment of her responsibility.

She could find unsuspected joys within the home: the closeness of a story hour with a small child, the delectable smell of her own bread as it emerges crisp and brown from the oven and the satisfaction of stitching up a new print dress on her own sewing machine. She may discover the smell of fresh earth in her own back yard, or if she lives in a city, transform her apartment into a greenery of growing plants and flowers. She can treasure the precious moments with her husband, catching up with his life and thoughts over a bedtime snack, laughing together over some ridiculous event. She also requires some outlet outside the home.

This disgruntled young woman is typical of many an American girl who must have her home and adventure too. She desires maternal satisfactions but clings to worldly pleasures. Why should American women, with the highest standard of living in the world, be at the same time among the most anxious, restless and dissatisfied women anywhere? They have more material abundance and freedom of choice and action than any women in the history of the world. Yet they are confused as to what should be their role, feel pulled and pushed by many conflicting demands, and yearn for still greater glories and satisfactions. The conflict is the result of the very freedom of choice. The woman of the past knew what was expected of her; the woman of today must decide for herself.

One housewife commented that when she felt a slave to her family she reminded herself that this was the responsibility which comes with deliberate choice. "No one forced me to get married. I asked for it," she declared. "Now it is up to me to make the most of it." In choosing to work for her family, this woman is illustrating both the freedom and the restrictions which accompany it. Without this structure of opportunity and consequence she would not be practicing free choice.

Every one of us occasionally makes a poor choice, or "wrong" decision, which we live to regret. One of the most difficult and challenging tasks of life is to live with our mistakes, to accept the results of our actions. It is not for us to turn away from the consequences, but to accept them with grace and courage. This is the internal freedom that brings a serenity of spirit which is inner-directed and not dependent on outer support. Its reward is a self-respect and personal dignity that cannot be bought or given.

Within us are unsuspected reserves of strength, but they must be cultivated. Katherine Mansfield, who died in 1922 leaving her noble contribution to the world in spite of terrible suffering, says in her journal: "I do not want to die without leaving a record of my belief that suffering can be overcome. For I do believe it. What must one do? Do not resist. Take it. Accept it fully. Make it a part of life. Everything in life that we really accept undergoes a change. This is the thing that in the greatest is a shining light, a pure white fire; and in the humblest is a constant gentle radiance, a quiet perpetual gleam. When we stop running away, when we really accept, that is when even tragedy succumbs to beauty."

Every woman comes upon painful times. She may feel abandoned by fortune or oppressed by circumstances. She may face loss and suffering in the family, a disheartened husband, disappointments within her marriage, intolerable living conditions or just an oppressive pointless boredom which she cannot shake off. It is then when she turns to a sort of elemental human guts which enables her to trudge on. She may be able to reach outside for help, to a friend with a sympathetic ear or to a professional counselor. She may make a bold decision or change of circumstances. Often there is no good solution, and like my mother who spent twenty-five years on a lonely and primitive farm on a river bank, she simply makes the best of it. This is no superficial pollyanna sunshine. This is the animal resilience which we all have buried within us.

What a furtive hope is pleasure. For life does not deal with us so tenderly as to cater to our personal desires. Life deals us a set of cards, and then says, "Here, see what you can do with them." To take an unbalanced or mediocre hand and play it brilliantly—this is what makes the game exciting. Even when choice seems nonexistent, life can be an act of declaration rather than the course of least resistance. One asks oneself over the morning dishes and in the dead of night, "What shall I do with my life?" If the answer is primarily a self-centered one, it is sure to be limiting and eventually unsatisfying.

If a woman matures as she ages, a time comes when she will put aside the wish, "Oh, what I long to be," and ask herself, "What does life require of me?" She ceases the yearning, "What would give me greatest pleasure," and demands of herself, "What is my responsibility?"

When she has decided what her responsibility shall be, she has also determined her goals, her purposes in life and her daily philosophy. It is important to think of responsibility in the broadest possible terms: family, world, community and self. It is helpful to think through one's philosophy in a fairly specific way. I have set forth my own thoughts in this way: "My purpose in life is to help make it possible for every living person (myself included) to develop his or her own potentialities in the greatest measure, and to live creatively according to his or her own possibilities." I work to achieve this in my personal family relationships, through my husband's work, through community service and in support of organizations and political candidates dedicated to this purpose on a national and international level.

When a woman has determined what shall be her goals in relation to her family, community and self, then she must think through the implications of these convictions and set her life accordingly. It is true that she will at times find her choices conflicting with the attitudes of those around her.

"We rented our house to friends while studying abroad last year," a young housewife in a Southern town told me recently. "Because these friends happened to be Negroes, we felt the wrath of the whole town come down on us. The white part of town, that is. We were cursed anonymously over the phone in the middle of the night, old friends refused to speak to us, neighbors were venomous, and a rumor was circulated that we were Communists. If my husband hadn't been employed by the federal government, he would surely have lost his job. It is frightening to have people hate you like that, yet we felt we were doing the right thing. We learned to accept the threats without flinching, and in the end felt stronger because of the experience. Our marriage took on a new dimension, too. It was as if we had found new resources to share with each other, and we felt close as never before."

This young couple had the courage which follows conviction. In acting on their beliefs they exercised both freedom and responsibility. We often think of freedom narrowly, as freedom from something, freedom from pressures or coercion. On the contrary, true freedom is an inner thing. It is a state of mind. It is a deliberate exercise of choice. Thus if we think we are bound by external forces, we are deceiving ourselves. It is our unwilling acquiescence to these outer demands that imprisons us.

At times a woman may have to temper her independent action with consideration of the needs of those around her; her husband's job, her children's well-being, a friend's future: all these may be at stake. She may also have to make compromises between her own goals and the prevailing attitudes of her culture. Then let her choose, but let it be a conscious compromise made for her own carefully considered reasons, and not a decision made for her by the pressure of outside opinion. The decision is an inner one, and this is the meaning of freedom.

Many married women are choosing to put their professional training to work in community service. More need to do so. Thankfully, our favored modern woman need no longer make an "either-or" choice between career and marriage. In fact, a woman's highest fulfillment lies both in being a mate and in making an independent contribution to society, either as an employed or as a voluntary worker. Our communities desperately require enlightened leadership. A woman's opportunities are like a smorgasbord laid before her, and she need only ask herself, "Where is the most urgent need?" With the help of a wise and sympathetic husband, she can blend the two and find the proper balance at any particular time in her life between service in the home and service in the community.

An attractive and intelligent young woman, upon graduation from an excellent liberal arts college, had this to say, "I have spent four years studying history, literature, and the arts. I want to teach dance to young people. I would like to open up to them the possibilities for self expression through the dance form, to enrich their lives. I have some ideas on relating the dance to the other arts that I would like to try out, modern dance with poetry, for example. I also share with many other girls coming out of our college, a sense of responsibility to our society. We feel we have an obligation to make a contribution, to give of ourselves to make the world a better place in which to live. We are trained to be leaders. Yet I want to marry and have a family."

Our college women are being trained in the arts and professions, and want to try out their skills. At the same time their physical and emotional needs press them toward marriage. For the highly trained professional woman it is a neat trick to compromise her maternal needs with the desire to express her vocational skills, but it can be done. It may mean stopping work entirely while her children are young, then picking it up part time when they reach school age. During the interim, she may be able to express her intellect and imagination by carrying on projects at home along the lines of her training. Indeed, the intelligent woman requires some such form of self-expression.

A former news reporter continues to write press releases for organizations to which she belongs, and short stories which she hopes to publish. A former actress plays in little theater. A woman trained in social work helped to organize a Fair Housing Practices Committee in her town and to work actively for racial integration. A former teacher serves on the religious education committee of her church and seeks to express religious ideas in dramatic form through church school work.

In research on careers for women, increasing attention is given to the emotional needs of women for the maternal role. As Amram Scheinfeld states, "There is a growing feeling that marriage and motherhood instead of always being obstacles to careers, may add to a woman's worth and chances of success by giving her greater stability, enriching her emotional life, broadening her interests, and increasing her understanding of people and their problems."[1] A study of brilliant professional women who had received their Ph.D. degrees from Radcliffe showed that the married women had surpassed single women in scholarly attainment, as judged by research publications.[2]

Helene Deutsch, in her book, *The Psychology of Women,* has described the "feminine core" of the womanly personality. She includes such qualities as "greater proneness to identifica-

[1] Amram Scheinfeld, *Women and Men* (New York, Harcourt, Brace, 1944).
[2] The Radcliffe Committee on Graduate Education for Women, *Graduate Education for Women* (Cambridge, Harvard University Press, 1956).

tion, stronger fantasy, greater subjectivity, inner perception and intuition." She believes that men tend to express their feelings through outward action, while women tend to direct activity inward, which gives them a rich emotional life. Feminine women have an extraordinary need of support when engaged in activity directed outward, but because of their capacity for identification they are able to inspire their men and rejoice in their husband's achievements. They are ideal collaborators and find greatest happiness as helpmates. Dr. Deutsch concludes that the "feminine core" forms "a nucleus that combines biologic, physiologic, anatomic, and psychologic elements resulting in a harmonious balance of passivity, masochism and narcissism."[3]

Esther Matthews has expressed the following theory of career development for women, based on her research and experience in career counseling:

1. "Men and women differ biologically, socially, psychologically, and intellectually." This genetic difference is usually disregarded, yet has profound implications for the education and vocational training of women.

2. "The deep and unchanging 'feminine core' of woman's nature exerts ever increasing pressure toward the solution of the marriage-career conflict in favor of marriage."

3. "The feminine core of a woman's life may be accepted, feared, repressed, denied, or sublimated." She may repudiate femininity and aggressively pursue a masculine career.

4. A woman who has not found feminine fulfillment in marriage may secure partial satisfaction through a nurturing vocation.

5. The intellectual creativity of many women "appears to be immobilized by the high level of diffuse anxiety generated by the partial or total lack of fulfillment of the complete feminine existence."

[3] Helene Deutsch, *The Psychology of Women: A Psychoanalytic Interpretation* (New York, Grune and Stratton, 1944, Vols. I and II).

6. "Women's unique intellectual productivity will be *fully* released only when basic feminine fulfillment precedes or accompanies her intellectual efforts."

7. "A profound understanding of women's personality dynamics may result in the ordering of a society in which women's fulfillment may be both as wives and mothers, and as intellectually creative individuals."[4]

Thus the young graduate who wanted both romance and dance may yet find them. After her babies come, she may lead motion choir in a church worship service, try dance therapy as a volunteer at a local mental hospital, or organize a mother-daughter class in her neighborhood. Perhaps by the time she is forty, administrators will have realized what a valuable pool of talent they have in mothers of older children, and she will take a part-time job in a school. And because she has had the experience of marriage and family, she will be a more productive teacher.

Running a household is not as unchallenging an occupation as many of us assume. A housewife confronts many difficulties which test her resourcefulness and emotional maturity. One of the more subtle pervasive pressures which we all face is to conform to prevailing community customs. We sense the expectations: how to dress, how to rear our children, how to keep the house, organizations in the community which should—or should not—be supported, and what attitudes one should hold. Whether or not a woman will decide to go along with these things depends on how much she wants to be accepted by those around her. If she feels that for the sake of companionship or for her husband's work that she must make compromises of her individuality, then let it be. But let it be done with clear head, without rationalization, without guilt and without grumbling. This is not al-

---

[4] This partial presentation of Miss Matthews' conclusions was derived from *Position Choice and Career Development in Men and Women: A Conceptual Framework,* Harvard Studies in Career Development, No. 8, David V. Tiedeman, Robert P. O'Hara, and Esther Matthews (Harvard University Press, Cambridge, Mass. 1960).

ways easy. Perhaps we make more compromises than we need to, however, for there is still considerable respect in our society for the strong, independent person.

A simple but practical example of this kind of accommodation occurred during the writing of this passage. A new neighbor had been invited for afternoon coffee on the day that the preschoolers in this house decided to rearrange the furniture to make a circus parade, with all their movable toys in the act. I believe that the children should be able to exercise their imagination freely in their own home. But the new neighbor is one of those immaculate housekeepers who feels positively uncomfortable in the midst of clutter. The solution in this case—to confine the rubble to the dining room and kitchen, and declare the living room "out of bounds." A planned pickup time followed the period of free play.

Another problem which bedevils the mother of young children is the twin torment of loneliness and lack of intellectual stimulation. With ingenuity, this can be partially overcome. A mother of twin babies, who had recently moved to a new community, encountered three other inquiring minds and formed a poetry-reading group. Later, she helped form a study group on comparative religion, with each member responsible for studying one religion intensively and leading the discussion for the group. A young woman with three vigorous little boys worked on the precinct level for the political party of her choice, and served on the board of the state chapter of the NAACP. Another housewife in a small town joined with a friend in starting a Great Books Discussion Group. A former music teacher with a two-, three- and four-year-old formed a chamber music group which met once a week, and also put on a benefit concert to raise money for the newly formed chapter of The Committee for a Sane Nuclear Policy, which she helped organize.

At this point many a mother with a new baby will throw up her arms in amazement and declare, "Impossible." She feels tired, pressured, on constant call and can never catch up with the tasks awaiting her. Perhaps being "caught up" is a luxury to be put aside while the children are young. I asked one busy, farm wife how she found time for outside activities. "I don't find time, I just *do* them!" she answered. The mother on duty day and night with toddlers and a new baby needs the outside interests more than ever. A sympathetic husband or a baby sitter several nights a week may make it possible for her to find the refreshment in mind and spirit which she so greatly needs.

When outside interests come in conflict with family demands, a woman may have to choose one or two projects on which to concentrate, and simply be resigned about the other attractive possibilities. For the family size will shrink soon enough, and then she can fill the vacuum with her manifold interests. No middle age readjustment for her—just the opportunity to start those postponed secret ambitions.

Lack of money is another irritant which seems to beset most households. This is often a problem of wants exceeding ability to pay. Newlyweds want to continue the standard of living they knew in their parents' home, yet their parents worked years to reach this level of income and accumulated goods. The appetites of the young couple are whetted by persons around them living high and fat, and the conflict within them is produced by the very possibilities of abundance. Yet even the most austere home today would seem a fairyland of plenty to the eyes of women in the history of the world, and to one-half the world's women today living meagre existences in peasant huts. Actually, a family can manage on much less income than one would expect. Our essential wants are simple, as the outdoor camper knows.

The use of low cost foods, such as dried milk, legumes, ground meat in casseroles, low cost fish and a few basic vegetables and fruits can, with careful management and a little ingenuity, provide a tasty and nutritious diet, and the occasional splurge for a roast makes a holiday the more festive an occasion. A family of moderate means can squeeze out extra money for symphony tickets, travel or other special events through careful food management. Another family may have to make a more radical change in their standard of living to be able to afford the kind of opportunities to which they aspire. This may mean moving to older housing in a less desirable location, making their own clothing or buying in markdown shops, finding used furniture through newspaper ads and auctions, and relying on buses and an occasional taxi rather than maintaining an automobile.

Another perennial problem is the near impossible task of remaining cheerful, patient and calm when overwhelmed with demands and irritations. On the same day that the washer is leaking and the oven is out of order, the baby is teething, the children are whining, a sick relative needs our care and husband will be home late for dinner. Then we can thank our good fortune for even having a washer, oven, child and husband. We can remind ourselves that in no place but in magazine ads are we promised that housekeeping is going to be entertaining and easy. Like every job, it has its drab chores and many strains, but it can have rewards all its own.

Chief among these is a mother's firm conviction that no task is more significant, no opportunity more precious than feeding the bodies and minds of those dearest to her. Her affection and companionship offer a supporting base for her husband, while her very presence gives her children stability. She teaches them the simple household ways and values which can transmit and enrich a civilization. Most valuable of all is her simple enjoyment of them. Feeling her pleasure and acceptance, they may begin to build the rock-like self-confidence and self-respect that is the core of integrity. Since integrity, like religion, is "caught, not taught," they respond to the strength within her. If she can impart some measure of self-awareness as well as sensitivity to others, and can excite their inquiring minds, who knows what greatness may lie in store for these children.

One writer considers as his original inspiration the time spent listening to his mother read aloud the poetry she loved. A musician remembers his mother's adoration for Bach. An athlete recalls the evenings after supper playing catch with his parents. The businessman feels, though he cannot specifically remember, his parents' pride in his ambition and vigor at school and in the alley.

Surely homemaking can be richly rewarding to the woman who accepts its limitations with patience and grace, and discovers opportunities all about her for personal growth and service.

WOMAN, THE TEACHER OF VALUES

Edith F. Hunter

Edith F. Hunter was graduated from Wellesley College and from Union Theological Seminary. Former Curriculum Editor for the Division of Education of the Council of Liberal Churches, she is the mother of four and author of several books including *The Questioning Child and Religion* and *Conversations with Children*.

He was five years old and his great-uncle was sixty-five. He lived on the East Coast and his uncle lived on the West Coast. They had never met before. They were becoming acquainted as they walked through a worn-out meadow in New Hampshire.

As they neared an old stone wall, badly in need of repair, the great-uncle said, almost to himself: "Something there is that doesn't love a wall . . ."

Startled, the one who was five, looked up and said, "Do you know Robert Frost?"

Equally startled, the one who was sixty-five looked down and said, "Do *you* know Robert Frost?"

"Oh yes," said five. "We have a whole record of him. My favorite is 'The Runaway.' You see, the baby horse didn't even know what snow was—and nobody could tell him, either."

There was a pause. "My sister likes the 'Hired Man' one best, but that's too sad. . . . You know he died."

"Yes," said sixty-five. "I know."

The five-year-old had as yet only a slim acquaintance with stone walls, snow and death. He, like the frightened young colt, had many things to learn, things that no one could tell him. The sixty-five-year-old had been developing his appreciation and understanding over a lifetime, through experiences, reading and reflecting.

The stretch of years between five and sixty-five (and actually, of course, before five and after sixty-five) is time spent incorporating into our private selves, the world into which we have been born. Each of us does this in a unique way, out of a unique life situation, and creates in the process one wholly new individual.

Both men and women live through the same cycle of birth, growth, maturity and death, but nature has, to some extent, circumscribed the context in which most women mature. Women always have, and I imagine always will, bear the children of the world. No culture has as yet worked out a variation on this.

It is a fact, therefore, that for a large portion of our maturity, perhaps twenty-five years, we will be living intimately with the children we bear. If we undertake the major care of the children before they start the first grade, and my premise is that the mothers should, we will have a great deal to do with the kind of persons they become and they will have a great deal to do with the kind of persons we become.

Sometimes, when we read of the plight of modern women, it sounds as if the primary problem facing us is that so many educated women are "ending up" in the home, instead of being out in the world doing something significant.

Educated women in the home! What an odd thing to deplore! What better place to have us "end up," although it might be more accurate to say "live," since children do usually grow up before we end up. What more important job is there than sharing the values we are learning to cherish with the next generation of adults? What more strategic place could there be for educated women?

> I don't care who you are, woman:
> I know sons and daughters looking for you
> And they are next year's wheat or the year after
> hidden in the dark loam.[1]

[1] Carl Sandburg, *Harvest Poems*, 1910-1960 (New York, Harcourt, Brace & World, 1960), p. 65.

Unfortunately, a widespread by-product of the higher education of women is the notion that an educated woman has fallen by the wayside if she is functioning full time as a mother, wife and creative woman in her home. An educated woman is considered a success, on the other hand, if she is doing research for a news magazine, laying out ads for underwear, engaged in further study or somehow employed outside the home.

A feature spread in one of the large private women's college alumnae magazines, entitled "Dust Mops or Dissertations?" is symbolic of this attitude. To weigh the scales even more than the title does, an editorial comment at the top of the page suggests that the author of "Dust Mops" was a rather typical young graduate because she showed "complete contentment with home, husband, children: with no intellectual yearning."

No intellectual yearning! The article was full of intellectual yearning, articulately expressed by the young author, but the yearning was being stimulated and nourished in the context of the home and community which apparently rendered it non-intellectual. The author of "Dissertations" on the other hand, was taking courses, which thereby indicated that she was doing something intellectual.

If the two articles had been presented with a different bias, the title might have read, "Dusty Dissertations or Living Spirits." Our colleges seem to encourage their graduates to think that they must return frequently to their alma maters in order to wipe the rust from their intellects. The colleges should be eager to cut the umbilical cords they so often seem intent on forming. They should seek to produce graduates who will find in every new experience a chance to grow and learn.

Instead, I have heard graduates of our finest colleges lament that they could not respond to a small son's interest in rocks, because they never took a course in geology, or to a three-year-old daughter's curiosity about plants, because they never "took anything like that" in college.

What makes us think that we can only learn something by taking a course in it? The best teachers in the world are children, and there are excellent books in even the smallest libraries now on such subjects as rocks and plants. The books written for eight- to ten-year-old children make ideal introductory material for parents who want to learn. To be sure, no professor has made the assignments and no credits will be given.

The education of women, I believe, should start with the statistically sound premise that most women will spend a major portion of their energies for fifteen to twenty-five years raising a family. For this job they will need the best training available. I do not think that we have any idea yet of what this training should be. Right here is a major assignment for educated women in the home.

If women were convinced, as a result of their own education, that the care they give their children in the first ten years of each child's life is one of the most important jobs that they will do in their whole lifetime, I think women, their husbands and their children would profit greatly. Instead, too many women, as a result of their formal education, are convinced that if they are staying at home with their children, they must be content to mark time in their own most potentially fruitful and creative years. Only when the children start school will they be able to live again. Many women, therefore, are responding to the advice that they have their children quickly and get that part of their lives over with. I think this is a serious mistake and families are the poorer for it.

What might a different attitude mean? How might it affect the children? We know that the first six to ten years are crucial in a child's life. We may even have read this in a textbook at college. We also know that when our children get to school the educational situation is rarely ideal. In all too many areas of the country the quality of those who can afford to teach is not as high as it should be. We know that classes are often too large and that there is little time to reach each child individually. In most school systems it is rarely possible to take the children on the excursions and field trips through which so much is learned. But look at the homes of a large proportion of our educated women! We have in them, very often, a fine educational setting. We have the pupils, our children, full time for the first five or six years of their lives. Why don't we put our buckets down right where we are?

Potentially, we have excellently trained teachers, ourselves, the mothers. Very often, as the suburbs expand, we have "classrooms" with easy access to the out of doors. City dwellers can capitalize on museums and parks and zoos. An increasing number of women have a car available all day. Labor-saving devices make it possible to dispose of housework quickly and easily.

In spite of the fact that families are becoming larger, it is rare that more than three pre-schoolers are home at one time. Here are the small "classes" our children need. These are the golden years for children's learning and educated women are in the key spot as teachers. What are we doing with the opportunity?

If we are doing more than just sitting out the years with our children or hiring someone else to sit with them, we are discovering that our life with them contributes to our growth as well as to theirs. Children, like artists, cause life for those around them to appear in fresh perspective. Most of us need this after sixteen years of an education mediated largely through books. Our children continue our education by bringing us into contact once again with the most elemental things, with the dramatic miracle of human growth as it goes on day after day.

Charlie, at one and a half, is the fourth great teacher I have had.

"Go get your boots," I say, when it is time to go out in the morning.

"Boots, boots!" he shouts, he squeals, he crows. He runs

and bounces out into the hall, and paws through a maze of larger boots, finally extracting his own small red ones. Clasping them lovingly to his breast he brings them back to me in triumph.

And where do Charles and his red boots take me in the course of our morning walks? We live in the country, in the Northeast. If there is snow, we must walk in it, kick it, scrunch it and crunch it. If there is rain, there are puddles and we must walk in them, stamp in them and splash through them. If there is mud we must know just how it feels under foot.

The red boots are apt to lead me across the meadow and down to the brook. Is the water high or is it low? Is there ice? Is the muskrat at home? We must throw in our quota of stones before going on. We may go to the woods for checkerberries and mushrooms. We may go to the chicken house to pick up eggs. We may go to a neighbor's to watch the baby have a bath. We may go to town and, if we are lucky, see that rapidly vanishing modern dinosaur, a train.

Wherever there is life, motion, activity, change, a child is drawn. We do not have to awaken his curiosity. This is natural to a small child; and along with curiosity, wonder and reflection. Already, a hundred times a day, I see a look cross his beautifully expressive face that says: "Wait a minute, let me feel that again. That's important. I want to think about that some more."

During these times with our children, we mothers receive as much and more than the children do. For we not only share with them the wonderful experiences with elemental things, but having lived longer, having some knowledge of other peoples and places, having entered further into our heritage of ideas and values, we are able to take a single experience and put it into a larger context of meaning and importance.

"All right," I said, "there's nothing in the road, let's cross over."

But no. He stopped. He stooped down on his haunches. He laughed. An ant, an infinitesimal creature was crossing our path. My eyes, adjusted to car-sized objects, of course had seen nothing. A line from Robert Frost flashed across my mind—"This was no dust speck by my breathing blown, But unmistakably a living mite . . ."

We watched it, together. He reached out that ever curious finger of the eighteen-month-old toddler, to touch it. Too little to know how fragile is the body that houses the life of an ant, I suggested he "love it," not touch it.

To "love it" for Charles means to lie with his face on the object being loved, so down he went. The ant, lucky this time, crawled safely out between his chin and arm while being loved. Although Charles was too young to know the difference between the living and non-living, this was a beginning acquaintance with a possible attitude toward living things. By suggesting he be careful and gentle with this tiny, moving thing, I was saying something about the value of life.

Hundreds of experiences later, by the time he is three, he will have a clearer idea of the difference between something alive and something not alive. Still more hundreds of experiences and thousands of words later, he will have some knowledge of the scientific, philosophical and theological ideas and controversies associated with the phenomenon of life. I believe that the walks and talks we have with our two-year-olds in red boots have a great deal to do with the values they will cherish as adults.

And these experiences are important to us, too. In college we were often given the world's best answers to all the great questions of life, but unfortunately, most of us had not lived long enough to have asked very many of the questions. But in the day-to-day experiences with our children, we begin to see life in full enough perspective to ask some of the great questions ourselves. Through our children we—fathers as well as mothers—have a kind of spiritual reprieve.

If the period of motherhood were approached with the attitude that we have much to give to children and much to gain from them, the dichotomy that is so characteristic of the lives of many educated women might be avoided. Being a good teacher to our own children takes a great deal of energy and time, but if we have direction and purpose, and plan our time wisely, we can be working toward three homogeneous goals. We can be laying the foundation of fine persons in our children, developing our own special skills further, and growing in sensitivity and awareness.

It was bedtime and the five-year-old philosopher of stone walls was now six. He was helping me with material for a book. We were talking about some of the things we like best.

Something in the conversation reminded me of Rupert Brooke's poem, "The Great Lover." I asked him whether he would like to hear some lines of a poem in which a man had listed some of the things that he loved most.

"All right," he said, "go ahead."

So I began.

> *These I have loved:*
> *White plates and cups, clean-gleaming,*
> *Ringed with blue lines; and feathery, faery-dust. . . .*

I paused. "I don't know what he thought was so pretty about dust. There's too much of that around!"

"Oh, I do!" said the little boy enthusiastically leaning forward. "You know the kind," and he brought his hand down hard on his bed. A cloud of dust rose up from the blanket.

"Don't you know how pretty it is when the sun is out and the dust rides up on the sunshine?"

"Oh yes," I said. "I'd forgotten about *that* kind."

I went on with the poem. There were many loves that he and Rupert Brooke had in common besides dust.

There was "the cool kindliness of sheets" and "the rough male kiss of blankets," and "grainy wood." He laughed when I said this because he has a large section of a cedar log in his top drawer. I have been instructed to drape his freshly ironed handkerchiefs over it in order to make them smell "cedary."

"The beauty of a great machine" brought an exclamation of delight since, that very day, he had seen a brand-new printing press at work. "It really was beautiful, too," he said.

In fact, he was so caught up in these shared loves that I said, "Wasn't it a good thing that Rupert Brooke wrote that poem? He knew that someday he would be dead, but he liked to think that these same things would go on being loved by a person like you."

"Is he dead?" came the surprised query.

"Oh yes," I said. "He died in the war that happened just before I was born."

"Did he get killed?"

"Not in the fighting. He was a soldier and he got sick and died. It was too bad, too, because he was very young and handsome. He wrote another poem that I always liked. It was about what he wanted people to think in case he did die in that war."

"Tell it to me," said the little boy, with a worried note to his voice.

Not sure that he would understand much of the poem, but sensing the urgency he felt to know exactly what this poet, who loved what he loved, wanted him to think, I began:

> If I should die, think only this of me:
> That there's some corner of a foreign field . . .

I stopped frequently, explaining various words, and continued with all of the poem that I could remember.

"That poem always makes me cry," I said, "because when Rupert Brooke wrote it, he didn't *know* he was going to die in the war, but when we read it, we know that he did die."

I noticed that his eyes were rather misty, too. "There's a nice idea in that poem," I said. "The idea that all the things we see and love as we're growing up, and everything that happens to us, becomes a part of us. We take all of these things with us wherever we go, even when we die.

"You'll take all the times you've flown kites, all the stories we've read, all the swims in the quarry, and even all the times we've talked like this together. And I'll take them too. When you're married and away, we'll both remember them sometimes and have them with us."

And there was a great big silence. The silence of somebody six years old thinking about such impossible times as when he'll be married or dead.

I pulled the sheets up around him and tucked the blankets in tightly.

"There's the 'cool kindliness of sheets' and the 'rough male kiss of blankets.' I suppose that when Rupert Brooke was a little boy his mother tucked him into bed. Someday you'll probably be tucking your little boy into bed and he'll grow to love the coolness of sheets and the roughness of blankets, too. That's nice to think about, isn't it?"

Through hundreds and hundreds of experiences like this values are shared, reflected upon and incorporated both by children and their parents. The home can be the seedbed of values, but it can only be this if someone is able and willing to spend the many, many hours that rearing fine people takes. The primary responsibility for this, I believe, falls naturally to women. Men can contribute richly, but they cannot make their unique contributions if women aren't making theirs.

What values do we women have to plant in this seedbed? When Charlie walks into the kitchen with his muddy boots *and* the first dandelions, which receives the major portion of our attention—the state of the kitchen floor or the first flowers of spring?

When we are reading a story to him and the telephone rings, do we always interrupt the story to give precedence to the telephone?

When we choose the storybook at the library, do we choose what is least boring to us or what delights him, although he has heard it a million times? Do we give any thought to the values that permeate the story itself?

When we buy him a toy, do we buy toy guns, handcuffs— whatever is the toy of the moment—or do we think about the values implicit in the toy? As the children get older, do we reflect on the values we are teaching by the daily newspaper we bring into the house, the magazines we put on the coffee table, the television we tolerate?

Are the friends we invite to visit, all of one skin color, one racial type, one social class? Does our conversation around the dinner table reinforce prejudices we are more or less consciously building up in our children, or do we try to open windows, prick curiosity, point out the ambiguities in so many of our political, economic and social problems?

A recent visitor at our dinner table sported a tremendously thick growth of beard, although he was not a "beatnik." He was an "idealist," and his analysis of our culture prompted him to lay all evil at the door of metal; he clearly articulated a desire to return to a Stone Age culture. For the older children, the dinner conversation and the conversations that followed after the guest had left, were as good as an introductory course on utopias.

For Charles the visit of the bearded guest had a value too, although a rather different one. The guest was seated next to him and in the midst of the meal Charles suddenly announced, as he often does when he sees that we have a good full table, "Hold hands."

He reached out a hand in each direction, one to me and one . . . he pulled his hand back . . . "Well,"—we could almost see him reasoning—"Well, I suppose that is a person behind all that trimming," and out went the little hand again. The unusual circle was complete and we sang the song we have composed to go with Charlie's ritual. All of us, including the guest enjoyed a silent chuckle over Charlie's obvious dilemma. In "one world" we need to be able to tolerate difference and Charles was beginning to learn this.

Education in values takes place in several contexts, and one of the most influential can be the home. I say "can be," because if we are never at home, or if the family is generally scattered, the effect families have on values will be dissipated. There is no substitute for the time parents spend with their children.

I have never forgotten some words I read by chance many years ago when I was a new mother. A woman who had achieved national prominence in the field of child development was asked what she would do differently if she had her life to live over again. She said that her one regret was that she had not spent more time with her children in their early years. She will never know how those words influenced at least one mother.

Charlie was all tucked in for the night and I was reading a story to the other three children. I was really reading to the six-year-old "great lover" who was now seven, but the thirteen- and fifteen-year-olds were listening, too. They had heard the story dozens of times before. It was the story of "The Richest King in the World," in which King Croesus is helped by wise old Solon to understand that material wealth is no guarantee of happiness.

When I finished reading, the fifteen-year-old, who had just written a report on *The Grapes of Wrath*, said, "Let me read you something. It says exactly the same thing."

Returning with the book, she found the place and read: "If he needs a million acres to make him feel rich, seems to me he needs it 'cause he feels awful poor inside hisself, and if he's poor in hisself, there ain't no million acres gonna make him feel rich."

If women can combine as their vocation and their avocation the transmission of values to each new generation of children, I believe they will be living the significant lives they so earnestly desire for themselves. Moreover, if they do this job well, they will know from the feeling of inner riches it gives them that what they have been doing has been of basic importance.

The result will be mature women, children with sound basic values and men who deeply appreciate their wives for having done this important job well. It will result also in a corps of women ready and trained to serve the larger community more fully in the next twenty-five years of their lives.

VOLUNTEER COMMUNITY WORK

Chase Going Woodhouse

Chase Going Woodhouse is the Director of the Service Bureau for Women's Organizations. She taught economics at Connecticut College and at Smith College and was a Connecticut representative to the United States Congress. She organized the Women's Division of the Office of the Military Government of the United States in Germany under General Clay, and served as Connecticut's Secretary of State.

The volunteer—an entire cross section of American life is embodied in these two words. Volunteer service ranges from giving a few hours to sort items for a thrift sale to devoting almost full time as vice-chairman of the national committee of one of our great political parties, or as chairman of a national voluntary organization. Each in its own sphere is important.

Foreign visitors, here to observe some phase of our industry, education or government, frequently comment on how much work is done by volunteers. "You mean, she gets no pay for all this?" is so commonplace a remark that it no longer surprises us. As one recent visitor said, "The willingness to work without pay, without apparently asking 'What will I get out of it?' reveals the social consciousness that has been built up in the average American woman."

Perhaps the lessons in what makes a democracy have sunk in deeper than we realize. Perhaps the pioneer tradition of usefulness, self-reliance, participation in the life of the community, is deep in us.

Both the community and the volunteer benefit. There is a great hiatus between the social needs of today and the availability of financial resources and personnel to meet them. Only the volunteer can make it possible even to hope to satisfy these social needs. We must be looking for ways to expand volunteer programs to include the participation of groups of people who have not traditionally been involved.

Some adjustments, for instance, will have to be made by the women's organizations in both program and scheduling of meetings to permit the employed women to participate. Furthermore, why must we think only of women as volunteers? Rightly or wrongly, many corporations and agencies retire men at sixty-five years of age. They still have years of usefulness. They can provide service to voluntary agencies which, in many cases, such agencies could not afford to buy.

And younger men are also a potential source. The work week is shorter. Young men are playing an increasingly active role in the family. It has been interesting to watch young men coming into the PTA, becoming officers, serving on community committees with representatives of women's organizations. After all, men and women frequently have the same interests. As more and more women enter paid employment, they have similar work experience and the same hours.

Again, why think almost exclusively of middle-class women as volunteers? In the days of a leisure class this was natural, but should it carry over into today? The wives of factory workers and women themselves working in plants are among the most devoted and effective volunteers in our political parties. And what of teen-agers? Can we not make them feel an integral and important part of the community? It takes planning to use them as volunteers, but there is much work they could do and, more important, the experience should develop a habit of volunteering which might carry over to their adult years.

Furthermore, such work enriches the life of the volunteer. One outstanding voluntary organization for young women states its purpose as "to foster interest among its members in the social, economic, educational, cultural and civic conditions of the community and to make efficient their volunteer service." The goals of this organization's training program, then, are twofold: to teach women how to effect changes within a community, and "to educate members for responsible citizenship . . . to develop each member's potential to the fullest . . . to train members for a mature citizenship through volunteer community service."

Our communities need the volunteer, and through her work, the volunteer develops into a more efficient citizen with a richer personal life.

Time was when a woman could not look to an active life that would last much beyond her child-rearing years. Now, however, once the children are out of the home for the major part of the day, most women will have at their disposal not only a great deal of time, but a great deal of energy, too. If these are to be happy, productive years, a woman must prepare herself for interests and activities based on her past job or her volunteer work.

Here are a few figures to ponder!

In 1900, a woman could expect to live to be 48 years old. Today her expected life span is 72 years. One out of every four women now aged 65 can expect to live an additional 15½ years. Of all persons who reach 65 years of age, 30 per cent of the women and 19 per cent of the men can expect to live to 85 years of age.

Since 1945, there have been more women than men in our population. By the year 2000, the estimates are that there will be 5 million more women than men in the 65 years-of-age-and-over group. On the average, a married woman can expect to be a widow for eight years.

With earlier marriages, the average woman has her youngest child in school by the time she is 32 years old, and out of the home when she is in the middle 40's. This leaves her a long time to go to the expected 72 or even 85 years! The wise woman will prepare. And volunteer interests are a safe hedge for well-being over those years!

Why Do People Volunteer? A number of interview studies have been made in an attempt to answer this question. The replies received list most frequently the desire to do something useful for others, community attitudes which attach prestige to volunteer work, the opportunity of meeting interesting people or sometimes just meeting people (a method of making friends in a new community, a problem facing many families with the mobility of company jobs), the inability to say "no," and personal interest such as better schools for one's own children. Then there is a negative reason. The social climate in some communities does not regard the woman "who doesn't do a thing" with much esteem. And the intellectual and emotional urge must not be forgotten. Fortunately there are people who feel so strongly about some social need that they go forth with the spirit of a crusader to alleviate the situation.

Americans have a genius for voluntary action, and for working together to gain the passage of important legislation. The work of many women's organizations just after World War II, in building understanding of America's new international position and responsibilities and of new ideas developed at Dumbarton Oaks and Bretton Woods, which eventuated in the United Nations and World Bank, is a notable illustration. We are all familiar with the government mutual security program, but it should be remembered that according to the best estimates there are at least 100 million Americans associated with voluntary agencies operating aid programs in many countries around the world—medical aid, education, techniques in agriculture, help for refugees, famine relief—and working in close cooperation with our government programs.

Many of these voluntary agencies, notably the missions, were operating such programs long before we were even talking about underdeveloped countries. They have performed two services: aid to the people of a less fortunate country in a way so direct as to establish the concept of the good will of the American people; and, in reverse as it were, they have brought home to many American communities a better understanding of and sympathy for these peoples of many lands. In brief, these volunteer "people-to-people" programs are genuine factors in the work for world peace.

Where to Volunteer. The field is wide. There is a place for everyone regardless of ability, degree of formal education, amount of time available and field of interest. The jobs which need to be done cover an immense range. They may be routine—addressing envelopes, answering the telephone, sorting and packaging. They may involve driving a car, visits to the aged, taking visitors to mental hospitals often difficult to reach by public transportation. There is need for teachers' aides, for persons who can lobby effectively, for service on policy making boards, for precinct workers, for candidates for office, for school boards and hundreds of other services. The foreign visitor program of the U.S. State Department depends on volunteers. In Connecticut, alone, the Service Bureau has the cooperation each year of several hundred men and women who assist the foreign visitors through home hospitality or by observation visits and interviews in their offices and plants.

The sensible volunteer relates her choice to her ability and training, to her reason for being a volunteer, to the time she can give, to her interest and to her family situation. She must be willing under some circumstances to take time to learn, perhaps to get training. Her choice should not consist in an act of conformity to a popular trend; (it is interesting to note that the number of volunteers in the heart and cancer campaigns is much greater than the number involved in mental health drives, though the social need is equally great).

It is well to look into the priority of needs in the community and to inquire where the greatest return for time is likely to be forthcoming. It is essential to know the make-up of the organization or agency and to be certain of agreement with its objectives before the volunteer offers her service. Then she should be certain she really understands what the job involves, the what, when, how and duration.

A part of the problem of recruiting volunteers rests on the professional staff. Perhaps one of the tasks which board members should attack more vigorously lies in this area of staff-volunteer relations. The staff has the responsibility of defining the job to be done, of placing each volunteer where she can be most effective, of providing the essential training, of making provision for necessary supervision, of taking time to show the volunteer how and where her specific job fits in as a part of the entire effort of the organization. The professional too must be conscious of the difference between her position and that of the volunteer. For the professional, the job has top priority. For the volunteer, while she must be responsible and dependable, family demands and family emergencies come first.

It is frequently difficult for a professional to admit that some phases of the job can be done by persons with less than professional training. It was not easy to bring nurses' aides into the hospital. Dentists were a long time accepting the dental hygienist. Today the question of teachers' aides can stir up a fine controversy, and the typical volunteer has less training than do these semi-professional workers. She must make allowances for this attitude and remember that professional standards had to be fought for and must be retained. But by doing a good job she can hasten the acceptance of the volunteer. In brief, both sides must maintain an atmosphere of flexibility, open mindedness, reciprocity and partnership, if the volunteer program is to be successful.

Public Affairs. For some individuals, work in public affairs may have more appeal than work in a voluntary agency devoted to a program in health, education or some other more or less specific area. The volunteer is an essential in public affairs. Our government is based on a two-party system, and to function successfully it must have the active participation of the great majority of the citizens. The volunteer is a key person whether he is president of a great industrial corporation relinquishing a stock profit of millions to serve his country in the President's Cabinet, or the quiet little woman over in a corner at party headquarters addressing envelopes. Both are important and so are all the volunteers in between. Without them we could not sustain a democratic government; we would be ruled by a bureaucracy.

Today, women account for 51½ per cent of all eligible voters. This right to vote was won by volunteers, at first only a handful of pioneers who faced ridicule and even abuse and who labored long and late. The story of these volunteers is dramatically told by one of them, Maud Wood Park, in *Front Door Lobby*.[1]

People ask, "What have women done with the vote?" This question implies a false assumption, and a crucial one—that women are a category rather than what they actually are, citizens differing one from the other just as men citizens do, some of them making good use of their vote, others uninterested or uninformed.

Although women have been exercising the vote for about fifty years, they hold only about one-half of one per cent of all elective and appointive officers. One reason for this is that women have felt that such work would interfere with family responsibilities. As we have seen, however, the possibilities of outside-the-home activities for women have increased tremendously since the time when women were first given the vote. Moreover, it is realized that women's participation in public life is not opposed to her responsibility to home and family.

When public office is mentioned people are apt to think of the U. S. Congress. Relatively few women have served in Congress, but those that have have served effectively, some of them over a long period of time. It would be difficult to conceive of a more satisfying job for a woman with the intellectual and physical stamina to face it. A congressman or a senator has the op-

[1] Boston, Beacon Press, 1960.

portunity to serve both the country as a whole and specific individuals, in a way open to few. It is not a glamour job! The hours are long; preparation for committee hearings are beyond what anyone has to do for a Ph.D. seminar; there are innumerable demands for individual service, for talks and reports to the constituents; and there is the necessity of determining each day how one should vote on measures covering a multitude of facets of our domestic life and international relations. There are also certain social demands which should be met, and congresswomen do not have wives!

However, one does not have to go to Washington, D. C. to play a useful part in public affairs. The state legislatures offer a wonderful opportunity dealing as they do with matters which affect so intimately and immediately many phases of family living. And in states like Connecticut, fortunate in being small geographically, the legislator can get home almost every evening.

Again, our city government, as has been so often said, is housekeeping on a great scale. The relatively few women who have been elected to city government offices have been able to accomplish a great deal. And still nearer home are boards of education and library boards, all needing able, active members. The statement that "politics are dirty" is one any real American should be ashamed to make. If, in a given community the statement is true, what has the speaker done to improve the situation? Let her who pulls her skirts aside be the first one blamed!

Holding office is for the few. But everyone should belong to a party, should take part in the party caucus, convention or primary and thus help nominate the best candidates for office. Some people take great pride in being independents, as if this gave them superior intellectual and moral status over a registered party member. As independents, they take no part in the nomination of candidates. They probably fail to realize that if we were all independents, under our form of government we would go to the polls on election day and find no names on the ballot, except in those few localities and for those few offices in which nomination by petition is permissible. In any case, everyone should keep well enough informed to make an enlightened decision on the major issues before our nation, state and local community. This is not always easy. One field in which volunteers are badly needed is in the improvement of our mass media.

Women have been the active initiators in many great movements for the bettering of life in America. It was Lucretia Mott and her volunteers who pushed the antislavery group in Philadelphia in 1833. Florence Kelly fought for the early legislation protecting both the worker and consumer. Jane Addams, Grace Abbot, Julia Lathrop, Mary Anderson, Agnes Meyer are all names emblazoned on the shield of great humanitarian movements.

Only a very few of us can achieve such heights of accomplishment, but we can work to safeguard a dangerous school crossing, to improve the overcrowded school bus situation, to help get out the vote, to help build up public opinion in favor of a needed zoning ordinance, to get the one gallon milk container approved, to list just a few of the dozens of opportunities for community service begging for action every day.

There is need for hundreds of women to work for better schools. The cold war is now a competition in brain power. Dr. Conant, in *The Child, the Parent and the State,* points out that "the upgrading of our schools cannot be passed on to the State Legislatures or to the U. S. Congress but rests on every citizen in the land" both as to finances and curriculum; the citizens "must get the facts about their local schools and then be prepared to go to work to elect a first rate school board and support its efforts to improve the schools."[2]

In brief, as Professor Stephen K. Bailey said at a Service Bureau meeting, "The responsible individual is one who budgets a part of her life to do battle, as a volunteer."

[2] James B. Conant, *The Child, the Parent and the State* (Cambridge, Harvard University Press, 1959), p. 83.

Who Are the Volunteers? The typical volunteer has been the middle-class woman with some leisure. Why is she becoming harder to recruit?

In the first place more and more women are joining the paid labor force. Today, we are in a competition of human resources. Our country needs the active, constructive, productive participation of every citizen, young, middle aged, old, man and woman.

There is no longer any question of woman's ability, of the desirability of educating her and of expecting her active participation in all areas of our economic and political life. In addition, society evidences a growing acceptance of the fact that women cannot be lumped together as a single category, that each is an individual differing from others in ability, training, interests, attitudes, physical stamina, mental stability and a dozen other traits.

Two important conditions, however, among others, still hamper our ability to recruit the most efficient working force. One is the problem of how to release women from certain family situations and community attitudes which prevent the full realization of their non-maternal capabilities. The other is the question of how clever a woman dares be.

Marya Mannes raised quite a storm with her two articles in the *New York Times Magazine,* "Female Intelligence—Who Wants It?" As she sums up the situation, "Women are not by nature denied the ability to think creatively and abstractly. It is rather that this ability is unpopular with women because it is unpopular with men. Our prior need, in short is to be loved . . . My point is . . . a woman who has the capacity and desire to think and to create in abstract terms should not only have ample opportunity to do so but the support of a society which needs all the independent intelligence it can get, man or woman." Miss Mannes points out that in spite of all the effort and money devoted in this country to the development of female intelligence, "every social pressure is exerted on women from their childhood on, toward a good marriage, the earlier the better—and babies, the more the better."[3]

Early marriages are interrupting the education of many girls. Large families demand all their physical energy and leave little strength for outside interests and little time for keeping up with the rapidly changing world, or for volunteer work.

The home is a very different place than it was a generation or two ago. Household help is almost nonexistent. Labor-saving gadgets help, but they do not provide the responsible person who must always be in a home where there are young children. The maiden aunt and the grandmother today both probably have jobs, or, with the mobility of our time are living miles away. The young mother has a lonely job in the home. Her day is full of deadlines—husband on the 7:20 A.M., first child on the school bus, second ready for the car pool to nursery school (or in her turn, tucking baby into a basket and driving the car pool), dancing class, Brownies, costume for the school play, etc., etc. Time for her own thoughts is hard to find.

And yet these young mothers want to be part of their community. Notably in the suburbs, they make heroic efforts to find time and energy for some club or volunteer work. A vague discontent and frustration is amazingly common among them. The world has changed so fast. Just a few years ago when they were in school going to the moon was a joke. The world is full of confusion, uncertainty and vague, unexpressed fears. Writers and speakers are attacking faulty value concepts in our social and economic lives. On every side parents are being told how to bring up their children. The father has more time to be with the children but the children are taken out of the home by school activities, Scouts, ballet lessons and other suburbia "musts" and, as they get older, by the automobile and a myriad of organized activities.

The pressure to conform, the competition for status, the neighborhood prescribed conventions of behavior and expend-

[3] January 3 and 17, 1960.

itures, all bear down on the family. However, the fact that our values or lack of them are being vehemently discussed by writers as different as Vance Packard and Walter Lippmann, and that people are reading what they write and some, at least, seem troubled by it, may mean that the situation will improve.

On my farm, the farmer and his wife work together at the barn, in the fields and in their home. On Saturdays and during school vacation the four children work with them or play within sight. The children are doing useful work or enjoying outdoor play. They create their own recreation. They do not have expensive equipment, and what the boy on the next farm has doesn't matter. Their lives are not organized. They are growing up to be self-reliant young people with skill and initiative. Comparing these children with those of friends in the city and suburbs one realizes what we have lost with the passing of the family farm. But it is an era which has gone. Young mothers are perhaps unconsciously struggling to find substitutes for the values the family farm used to engender, for not only have the situations of child rearing changed, but the fundamental attitudes and aspirations of the mother have been refocused as well. She is no longer sure what behavior is considered right and proper for her. She is deluged with exhortations in regard to her role as mother. The community demands her time for volunteer project after project. Public commissions tell her her work is essential in the American labor force. A few voices tell her that she is an individual, that what is right for her may not be right for some other women, that she must make her own decision as to her role. Yet, if she is employed outside the home, or is an active volunteer, she often is troubled, has a vague feeling of guilt, fears she is neglecting her family. And if she does no community work and devotes all or nearly all her time to her family, again there is a guilt feeling that she is shirking her duty as a citizen.

Somehow we have to cease regarding married women as a class apart and see each as an individual. Homemaking is coming

to be regarded as a job for both parents. Dr. Florence R. Kluck-
hohn has said it well: "To me, the serious problem in the family
situation of the United States is defining masculine and feminine roles in such a way as to let us break through the tendency toward segregation and have a more satisfying husband-
wife relationship."

There are many fine young women anxious and able to
serve their communities. They do not resent their household
tasks but they long for some time to be themselves, not just
"mother," to develop their own thoughts and interests. The
community demands their services, yet when has a community
given serious thought to making adjustments which would
give these young women a block of free time. Should it not be
possible to arrange school schedules so that no young mother
would have three young children each on a different school day-
time schedule with resulting school bus and car pool complica-
tions extending over morning and afternoon?

What is the objection to properly administered child day-
care and after-school centers run on a flexible basis and not at
the almost prohibitive rates of the private nursery schools, which
would allow mothers a whole morning or a day off every so often?
In a recent issue of *The Ladies Home Journal* Dr. Spock
compared the behavior of American and Russian children with
the balance rather in favor of the Russians. I have visited a number of day-care centers in the Soviet Union and agree with the
statements in this article. One can highly disapprove of the political and economic ideology of the Soviets and still see the good
in some of their institutions.

At the National Conference on Day Care for Children,
held in Washington, D.C. on November 17 and 18, 1960, one
speaker noted "that Day Care is too often regarded as a service
that should be used only when all else fails . . . Perhaps the
reason for our apologetic attitude is that we are reluctant to face
the reality of a society that has invited women to leave the home."

This conference formulated a set of excellent standards for day-care centers apparently solely with the employed mother in mind. Such centers might also relieve other young mothers for certain limited periods of time.

People who shudder at the mention of publicly financed day-care centers other than the semi-philanthropic ones for the very low-income working mother are frequently among those sending their children to an expensive nursery school. In England, the nanny, the governess, the boarding school for even the nine-year-olds have not destroyed the fiber of the nation. Many of today's grandmothers and even mothers were brought up in typical American homes with a full-time, live-in maid and often a nurse who spent a great deal of time with the children. The idea of a mother on twenty-four-hour duty is a recent development. We constantly retool and reorganize our factories to meet new situations. Why don't we apply our social engineering know-how to the problems of household and child care? It is high time that we stopped lecturing the young married women on what she ought to do and turn our attention to making it possible for her to do some of the things the community needs and for which she would like to volunteer.

These young married women are the rich source of the needed volunteers. They are the women who must provide the leaders for the social movements of the next decade. And for their own sake, they should be developing interests and activities to support them through the years after the children are all out of the home.

American women have been leaders in many a crusade of world import. Eleanor Roosevelt is without question the greatest and most beloved volunteer in the world today. American women have education; they have material facilities; they live in a free atmosphere. The focus of their lives must remain the home, but the home changes as the world changes and it can only be the haven it should be if women are in a position in which self-development is possible, in which they have some time and energy to work for the betterment of their community and of the world situation.

Children can share in the excitement of "mother's work." It is interesting to note the pride children take in mother's activity, if they are brought into it. Recently, I was in a home where two boys, ten and twelve, very promptly cleared the dinner table and did the dishes, explaining that on Wednesdays they hurried because it was "Mother's board night" and they knew she felt better if everything was washed and put away before she left. There was no question of the pride they took in her position on the board.

Employment of Women Outside Their Homes. While family and household situations make it difficult for young married women to volunteer, an important factor in the growing scarcity of volunteers among older women is the increasingly large number of women, and notably of married women, in paid jobs. Cynthia Wedel, in a pamphlet, "Employed Women and the Church" writes: "The structure of church organization and life, which, especially in America, has looked to women for much of the day to day work of the church, will be drastically affected by the changing role of women." [4] The same is undoubtedly true of other voluntary organizations.

Here are some figures which illustrate the trend. Between 1950 and 1956 the number of men employed increased by 3 per cent, the number of women by 17 per cent. Women now comprise some 36 per cent of the working population. It is estimated that the average young girl of today will work a total of twenty-five years over different periods in her life.

The number of women aged 35 to 50 holding paid jobs increased 60 per cent from 1940 to 1950, while the total number ber of women in this age group increased only 17 per cent. The average woman worker today is over 40 years of age.

[4] Cynthia Wedel, *Employed Women and the Church* (New York, National Council of the Churches of Christ in the United States, 1959), p. 5.

Approximately two-fifths of all women workers are 45 years of age or older. Approximately one-half of all women 45 to 54 years old are employed, and by 1970 it is predicted that 55 per cent of this age group and 43 per cent of those 55 to 64 years of age will be in the labor force. Excluding teen-agers and women 65 years of age and over, at least two out of every five women will be in paid employment.

Further, one-third of all employed women have children under 18. There are 2½ million working women with children under six. About 40 per cent of all married women are gainfully employed during the first year of marriage. This falls to 30 per cent in the second and third year. Put another way, three out of every ten married women are employed, and likewise, two out of every five mothers with children of school age. In addition, there has been an increase in the number of mothers of school children employed part time.

Why are these married women, many of whom in the past would have been volunteers, entering paid employment? Some reports explain it as the need for more income. Without question in low-income families, the mother's wage is essential. Families in more comfortable circumstances often desire to maintain a higher standard of living, to provide more facilities for the children.

One hears of tension and discontent among well-to-do wives of suburbia—the pressures of the household; the pressures of social demands; the insistent calls to help with this or that in church, Scouts, League of Women Voters, PTA and others, all deserving of help. Compared to the paid job so many of them had before marriage this is pandemonium! Labor-saving gadgets and careful planning, simply cannot eliminate all the tension. A paid job with regular hours, even if it takes all the pay check for help in the house, is a temptation. Automation, with its predicted shorter workday and week, will result in the employment of more married women.

A study of 200 upper-income women living in Westchester, New York, recently made by Mrs. Nannette E. Scofield brought out some interesting information. There were 62 per cent doing volunteer work but more than half wanted paid employment, 13 per cent immediately, the others in from five to fifteen years. Only 32 per cent were certain they would never seek a paid job. These women were realistic. Among them, 75 per cent felt their education was inadequate for the work they would like to do, and of these 85 per cent had plans to return to school. Most of these women held volunteer work in fairly low esteem.

Regardless of why more and more married women are in paid employment, the trend is recognized as here to stay for the foreseeable future. The National Manpower Commission declared that women's participation in production and in professional work is essential to the nation's economy and security. At the Arden House Conference, Harriman, New York on October 24, 1957, the ninety men and women representing business, industry, education, labor, child welfare and religion, after five days of discussion, concluded that the social and economic effects of the wider paid employment of married women are largely desirable and that the job trend will continue, because, without women in the labor field, we could neither produce and distribute the goods nor provide the educational, health and other services which characterize American society. Discussing some of the criticism leveled against the employment of married women, it was pointed out that juvenile delinquency cannot be laid at the door of these women, that it is a much broader question and that no social problem arises from a single cause.

In *Goals for Americans,* the Report of the President's Commission on National Goals,[5] the few references to women are all made in connection with the need for woman power. Dr. Wriston writes: "The fullest development of every individual is hindered by underestimating the potential of a majority—

[5] New York, Prentice-Hall, 1960. Reprinted by permission.

women . . . At a time when women constitute nearly a third of the labor force, it makes no sense from the standpoint of an expanding economy, to apply social sanctions which limit their earning power and deprive the economy of their executive abilities, their capacity for scientific research, and even their higher technical skills. The union of family life and careers is possible to a degree never before conceivable. Yet barriers of pride and prejudice are needless hurdles for women to surmount." [6]

And again, in discussing goals in education, John W. Gardner devotes a paragraph to the education of women. He deplores the fact that while women have entered the labor force in increasing numbers and now comprise 36 per cent of all workers, their rate of entry into the professions has declined. While 30 per cent of the B.A.s granted each year go to women, they earn only 10 per cent of the Ph.Ds. "Women should be encouraged to enter every field requiring advanced training. A woman's family obligations may make it necessary to modify the pattern of graduate and professional training established for men. Her professional career may also involve departures from the masculine norm. Colleges and graduate schools should make it easy for women to continue their education part time (or interrupt it) during the period of heaviest family obligations."[7] (It should be noted that Radcliffe College, Sarah Lawrence College and the University of Minnesota are pioneering in this area.)

Dr. Warren Weaver in the chapter, "A Great Age for Science," refers to women as "the lost half." "The biological facts must be conceded; but other nations are making it clear that it is possible to make adjustments to these biological facts and give women full opportunity for creative careers in science. . . . As the pressure for able personnel increases we simply must create new and appropriate opportunities for women." [8]

[6] *Ibid.*, p. 54.
[7] *Ibid.*, p. 84.
[8] *Ibid.*, pp. 115, 116.

In brief, women are needed in the labor force, in the higher ranks as in the lower. Yet there was no woman appointed to the Commission, and on only two of the fourteen panels was there a woman member (Culture, and Human Needs). Nor was any mention made of means to make it possible for women to adjust home and job. The statement, "Our goal must be to apply new technology so that it will improve the way men live and work." [9] apparently refers only to industry. This problem of lightening household cares must be given serious thought if women are to do all that is expected of them. And, as noted above, this applies to volunteer work as well as to paid employment.

Eventually, some way must be found for providing some free time for the young married woman. But this will not be done tomorrow. Meantime, the woman in her early forties is the one who must be "caught." With all her children in school when she is in her thirties she has some free time, and leaders of our voluntary organizations should be alert to finding promising volunteers in this age group. By not trying to overload them at first, it will be possible to build up a corps of full-time volunteers for the future.

The need to develop leaders of voluntary organizations was the basic reason for the establishment of the Service Bureau for Women's Organizations sponsored by the Beatrice Fox Auerbach Foundation. It works with seventeen cooperating organizations, (women's organizations which have national and Connecticut headquarters and at least five branches in Connecticut). Its purpose is to assist these organizations in developing leaders among their members and to help them implement their programs. It provides forums, seminars and dinner meetings in the fields of international relations, education and welfare and classes on organization procedures and techniques. Its various committees and subcommittees, well distributed over Connecticut, are on the constant alert for potential leaders.

[9] *Ibid.*, p. 196.

If the leaders of an organization make people feel they are needed, that they have something to give as well as to gain by working in the organization, if the program is worthwhile and if there is opportunity for training, membership will grow and active participation increase.

America, as the symbol of the free world, is faced with a mighty task. We have to set an example in meeting our social needs. We want peace, freedom, justice, a world in which all peoples will live together in harmony and cooperation. To gain such a world we have to make wise use of all our resources and especially of our human resources, of which the volunteer is an important factor. We must develop means of making it possible for more of our people, men and women, single and married, young, middle aged and old, to play a part as volunteers in meeting the social needs of our day at home and abroad so that at least the first steps can be taken toward a world at peace.

III. Women at Work

WOMEN IN THE PROFESSIONAL WORLD

Ethel J. Alpenfels

Ethel J. Alpenfels is professor of anthropology at the New York University School of Education. She received her B.A. from the University of Washington and her Ph.D. from Colorado State College of Education. Under a Rockefeller Foundation grant, she did extensive research among the Modoc Indians. She conducted a three-year research project on "Will Facts Change Attitudes" under the auspices of the National Conference of Christians and Jews. Her most recent books are *Sense and Nonsense about Race* and *Brothers All*.

> *Alice in Wonderland asked: "Would you tell me, please, which way I ought to walk from here?"*
>
> *To which the Cheshire Cat replied: "That depends a great deal on where you want to get to."*

The professional woman in the United States, like Alice in Wonderland, does not know which way she *ought* to go nor where, ultimately, she really wants to *get to*. To complicate matters even more, the surge of women into the labor force has buried, deep within a mass of statistics, any indication of where the professional woman *stands* and what is happening to her today.

In the revolution that has been taking place in the employment of women, the professions have attracted over 2 million women into occupations listed as professional, technical and kindred workers. Four out of five women are concentrated in seven professions: teaching, nursing, music, social work, accounting, auditing and library work. In other, less traditional fields for women, 6600 are engineers, 9000 are bank officers, 1000 hold high civil service positions and some 150 are foreign service officers.

These statistics and many others are often quoted and are well known to the sociologist. Less well known is that the professional woman, while increasing in actual numbers, is steadily declining in the relative percentage of the total professional class. In 1930, she made up 50 per cent of all professional and semi-professional workers. Now, in the 1960s, she constitutes less than 35 per cent. Why is this happening? Why is the proportion of professional women declining while, at the same time, the percentage of working women goes up, up, up, and the number of women in the total population of the United States exceeds the number of men by 2 million?

First, there is the potential loss of women workers arising from marriage, childbearing and child rearing patterns which must, of course, be reckoned with, for motherhood remains exclusively a women's profession. These work "disabilities" peculiar to women, however, have not reduced their population in the professions as much as in other types of employment. In certain professions—writing, music, publishing and medicine— women, like men, have not allowed physical handicaps or societal pressures to keep them from continuing their careers. In other professions, as in nursing, teaching and social work, women are able to resume active work soon after childbearing. For women who are college graduates, the pull toward work outside the home has for decades been greater than for those who are not college educated. A trend toward combining homemaking functions with employment, the number of women who return to their jobs as soon as their children enter school, accounts for the high percentage of women who perform the dual role of mother and career woman. On the other hand, there are professionally trained women who have been too long away from their jobs; many who find professional re-education or legal requirements too difficult; many who too easily abandon aspirations and, therefore, settle for something less than they once dreamed,—these are the women who account for a heavy loss of women from the ranks of professional workers.

Secondly, the continuing drop in the proportion of women to men in professional occupations results from the rapid expansion in scientific and technical fields which were almost unknown before World War II. They require special training and new technical skills considered to be outside women's traditional interests or capabilities and, too frequently, inappropriate or unnecessary in the education of girls and women.

Third in importance and, in the long run, a factor likely to be significant in the careers of women, is the change in men's attitudes toward what has traditionally been labeled "women's work." For better or for worse, men are now entering occupations formerly dominated by women. Teaching in the primary and secondary schools which, even as late as 1959, was described as "exclusively a woman's profession" has, in reality, been infiltrated by more and more men since the end of World War II. Concrete evidence, though entombed in statistical tables, indicates that long-held prejudices about the kinds of work thought appropriate *only* for women are now, slowly but surely, beginning to break down. In social work, in library science, in dietetics and nutrition and even in the nursing profession, "women only" labels are disappearing before the onslaught of a whole new generation of young men.

Public school teaching best illustrates what is taking place. For the first time in almost one hundred years, more men than women are on the teaching staffs of our high schools. At the elementary level, long the stronghold of the female schoolteacher, the proportion of men to women has been steadily climbing during the past two decades. Special inducements, like higher salaries, recruitment campaigns, promotion to administrative ranks and public approval, have succeeded in attracting and keeping young men in the teaching profession. This has also brought about drastic changes throughout the profession for women as well as for men. To keep pace with the cultural advances in other institutions and with our expanding economy, many of these changes were inevitable.

The strength of the tradition that primary and secondary schoolteaching are feminine occupations has not dissuaded men from entering them. It gives better balance to education. It is as good for little girls as for little boys. At the same time, however, men brought with them the practise of entering, not at the bottom, but at the top of the professional hierarchical structure. This is one of the factors responsible, not only for the decline of women in the professions, but for an uneasiness and growing frustration among many working women.

Originally welcomed as elementary teachers to offset, in part, the effects of "momism" and to provide masculine models for growing boys, men have remained to perpetuate the stereotype that leadership and administrative aptitude are not human qualities found in gifted persons, but are the property of the male sex alone. A young man and a young woman, with comparable education and skill, starting together as elementary teachers soon give proof, if proof is needed, that the man will rise more rapidly, receive a higher salary sooner, and that he will be given both the encouragement and the opportunity to do so. This is possible because today, as older women principals retire, they are replaced by men. In community after community, especially in the suburbs, the "lady" school principal is disappearing and men are taking over the administrative posts which were once the ways by which a woman achieved a higher salary, a promotion and a higher status. Everyone has heard the arguments, the financial and power urges that are used to support this kind of discrimination. There is no need to repeat them here. There is need, however, to ask not only what this personal and professional loss means to the women on the job, but what it means to the image of the "feminine" model for little boys and little girls?

Whatever answer society may give to that question, the crucial fact is that men's increased willingness to abandon time-honored sex labels attached to women's jobs has not been matched by the disappearance of "men only" tags attached to

masculine professions. There were 208 women listed among
the 6597 members of the American Institute of Physics, but
one-half of them are employed in the teaching profession; 6600
women are among those classified as engineers and other technical fields, but this is a tiny percentage in a profession which
numbers over 600,000; more women are to be found in chemistry—about 7 per cent are women—but, again, over half work
in the manufacturing industries; and some 3 per cent of all dentists are women.

Higher education best illustrates the special problems that
face a woman who seeks to enter the male-dominated and male-
oriented professions in the 1960s. Theodore Caplow, in his
book, *The Academic Marketplace,* does not mince words on the
subject of women in higher education. "Women scholars," he
writes, "are not taken seriously and cannot look forward to a
normal professional career . . . because they are outside the
prestige system entirely. Being outside the prestige system, they
cannot hurt . . ." or be a threat to men.[1]

In this penetrating report on the folkways and mores of
the academic marketplace, Caplow thereafter makes his point
about women scholars most effectively by completely ignoring
women in higher education. Thus, unconsciously but no less
effectively, he puts his finger on what may well be the crux of
the problem for professional women: *that in the world of
"ideas" women simply do not count.*

Unlike Professor Caplow, most men in higher education
seem unaware that women are outside the rigid caste system of
the academic world. Indeed, men at the top of the intellectual
pyramid are constantly reminding women that they are not
matching their male colleagues in scholarly research and publication. What they fail to recognize is that the fault may lie,
in part, in the discrimination that comes,—not because women
are newcomers to the academic world, not because as women

[1] Theodore Caplow and Reece J. McGee, *The Academic Marketplace*
(New York, Basic Books, 1959).

they have low status,—but because women have simply never been inside.

Whether recognized or unrecognized, this powerful and persuasive ghost sits at every conference table, in every committee meeting; it hovers in lecture halls and in counseling offices, and is part of the college woman's experience, day in and day out. In a thousand subtle ways, a young woman learns that women are less capable, less intelligent, less serious and less important than men. It propels her toward "soft" courses, pushes her into "women's" occupations and away from science and, finally, closes the door on many kinds of work for which she may be well suited.

Statistics in higher education support this generalization. Newcomers to the world of the "scholar," women soon dominated the early normal school. Today, they number one-third of the teaching staffs in colleges of education. In positions of educational leadership in *any* type of college, the relative percentage of women is now less than it was ten or twenty years ago. Four out of five of the full-time faculty in *all* types of institutions of higher learning are men. In private colleges, including women's colleges, women now represent only 14 per cent, less than it was twenty-five years ago. The dean of women is quietly but rapidly being replaced by the male dean of students. Promotion to full professorship, if given at all, goes to "home economics" or "nursing" departments. In one large university not a single full professorship has been granted to a woman in the last five years in those broad cultural areas which are required for graduation by all college students: the biological and physical sciences, the classics, philosophy, history or sociology.

Thus, the number of women teachers and administrators in higher education drops at precisely the same time as more and more women are expected to enroll in colleges. The New York University *Alumni News* of December 1961 notes that the enrollment of women has increased since December 1960 by 10 per cent. The status of women deteriorates even while

the administrative heads of their universities and colleges ponder the ways and means of salvaging lost talent and alleviating
the shortages of "manpower" in strategic fields. Leaders from
both within and without administration are maintaining,
through their own discriminatory acts, the fiction that women
lack the stability, the intellectual curiosity, the knowledge or
the ability to teach adults certain traditional subjects—much less
to assume academic or administrative leadership.

Is it any wonder, then, that college graduates, in their
later professional work, continue to perpetuate the stereotypes
which the male scholar destroyed through his own research?
College administrators, if they are really serious, can no longer
escape their responsibility. A little housecleaning is in order.

To suggest, however, that men alone are responsible for
the plight of women, or that all that needs to be done is to re-
orient men's thinking, smacks a little too much of the militant
early struggle for women's rights. Many women in higher education and in other professions, women with special talents or
with hidden drives or through dedication, have and are achiev-
ing positions of status in certain areas of the academic and professional world. But they do so at a very high price. It is not with
these women that the problem is concerned. The problem is
that the end product of this prejudice, more powerful because
it is so subtly exercised, is deleterious not only to women in
higher education but to education and to society itself.

The professional woman, on the other hand, dare not let
personal experiences and obvious examples become a mandate
to sit back and wait for someone else to take over. She has done
it for too long already and she must, like Alice in Wonderland,
begin to ask herself where it is she hopes to get to. This becomes imperative when one realizes that among *women* workers, the professional women represent "a smaller portion of
those segments of the labor force than they did a quarter of a
century ago. "In 1930, 15 per cent of all women who worked
were to be found in the professional and semi-professional occu-

pations." [2] In the 1960 census, only 10.9 per cent of the working women were so classified even though occupations, which had never before been considered sufficiently important to be listed, were each employing from 5000 to 50,000 women.

It is clear that the professions are claiming relatively fewer women than they did in the past, while the general fields of employment outside of the home are utilizing more and more women. Where are the professional women going?

The major direction of this exodus of women is toward occupations classified as clerical and kindred workers. Of women with from one to three years of college education, 36 per cent are professional, 36 per cent are clerical and the other 28 per cent are distributed among sales, managerial work and other occupations. Of all women with four or more years of college education, 16 per cent of them are holding clerical jobs. Since clerical work is the principal siphon of potential professional workers, examination of the drawing power of clerical work may offer clues to the goal considerations upon which working women operate.

For college educated women, secretarial work has always offered certain opportunities and, according to traditional rumor, has been the springboard via which a woman moves from clerical to professional status. A few talented women have, indeed, moved on to professional and executive jobs in book publishing, banking, in the great foundations and in the editorial, radio and television fields. More often, however, reality denies the myth. The high recognition given the successful secretary and the satisfactions she derives from being closely identified with the successes of her employer often combine to forestall her desire to move from the clerical to the professional category. The stereotype of the American woman as the helper to the man is perpetuated and, besides, it is both comforting and safe.

In addition, a topflight secretary can earn a far higher

salary, face less competition because of personnel shortage and achieve goal satisfactions more frequently than does the professional woman. It is easier, also, for the experienced typist to return to work after a long absence with less re-preparation than is necessary in professional fields.

In contrast, the professional woman in our society must constantly prove herself and, for most, recognition is at best both temporary and elusive. Consequently, recognition does not bring with it the deep satisfactions experienced by the skillful, highly qualified and dedicated secretary, not even those satisfactions to be derived from material gain. Surely if more women are to be encouraged to make long-range plans for careers in the professions, where the most acute labor shortages occur, then society must accord the professional woman as much opportunity for self-realization and satisfaction of needs, both personal and material, as society makes available for its secretaries.

The Image. As with most groups whose minority status has been confirmed by society, the female stereotype provides the *image* which the professional woman has of herself. This was reflected in a recent opinion poll conducted by the writer. Four hundred men and women from Newark College of Engineering and New York University were asked to list (1) the qualifications needed by men and women in the same professions, (2) the qualities and personality traits of the professional man and woman, and (3) to rank, in order of importance, ten careers for women. Two professions predominated, one-third of the respondents were engineers, one-third teachers and the remaining one-third came from communications, the arts, business and various health fields.

Qualifications. The women made sharp differentiations between the qualifications needed by men and those needed by women in the same professions. Men saw fewer differences in the necessary qualifications. Generally, however, both men and women stressed personality and human relation skills as most important for the woman, while education, training and work

skills were considered the predominant qualifications seen as
necessary for men.

Sixty-two per cent of the women saw themselves as *intelligent* but only one per cent listed education as one of the necessary qualifications for the professional woman. Seventy-five per cent of the men listed *education* for women but only three per cent mentioned intelligence as among her qualifications.

Only one woman said that a requirement for a professional woman was to belong to professional organizations, but not one mentioned professional reading as essential. Many women, however, saw this as a necessary professional requirement for men. Approximately 30 per cent of the men included this requirement for both men and women.

Eighteen per cent of the men mentioned that women should be young and single to qualify as professional workers. Only two women made mention of age, listing "below 50" and "around 42" as preferred qualifications.

Qualities and Personality Traits.

As respondents described the qualities and personality traits for professionals, the description of women's traits was much more diffuse and confused than that of the professional man. Only twenty qualities were mentioned as descriptive of professional men, while sixty qualities were invoked to describe the professional woman. The most consistent portrait of the woman was one of *inconsistency*. Both men and women rated aggressiveness as a leading characteristic of the woman, but gentleness, warmth and understanding were also a significant part of the profile. The woman was viewed as possessing leadership qualities, but is cunning, a manipulator and "uses sex artificially to play up to men." She is interested in world affairs and aware of others, but these qualities do not prevent her from being narrow in outlook, more concerned with home problems than with her job, dogmatic and autocratic. Women are sticklers for ethical behavior, but cold, hard, insecure and selfish.

Ranking of Careers for Women. In ranking the professions

for women there was an overwhelming tendency to consider the jobs which women should seek as those traditionally regarded as women's occupations. Men, however, named fifteen careers not mentioned by women, all of them in scientific and technical fields. Men saw more career opportunities for women while women clearly demonstrated a need to re-evaluate those occupations in which they might participate.

The five qualifications for the professional man, (appearing from 50 per cent to 100 per cent of the time on both lists) were: (1) education, (2) professional membership, (3) professional reading, (4) training and (5) personal appearance. Of these five, only personal appearance was considered equally important for women. An examination of the professional fields, however, indicates that the other four qualifications do have a great deal of bearing on a woman's success.

1. Education. For women as well as for men, this is the key factor in determining whether or not a woman is employed in a professional capacity. Only 60 per cent have from one to eight years of college education and "nine times out of ten she has been educated in a small co-educational college. Eight times out of nine she is from the white-collar group, and she is part of the 35 to 50 per cent of the high school graduates who have had education beyond the high school in training for her profession." [3]
2. Professional membership. The typical professional woman belongs to two organizations while in certain professions the number rises to five, including local, state and national affiliations.
3. Professional reading. Women subscribe to, although there is no certainty that they read, some three professional journals and, here again, the number rises according to the profession. This includes only those women who subscribe in their own names, and does not give any indication of what married

[3] Kate Heuner Mueller, *The Cultural Pressures on Women* (Washington, D.C., American Council on Education, 1959), p. 50.

women may subscribe to with their husbands or of what she
may read through office subscriptions.

4. Training. The average time spent by women in professional
   schools or in specialized training for certain professions is
   two years beyond high school. As for men, legal requirements and several highly technical professions which require
   excessive training sharply alter this figure.

5. Appearance. Men were overwhelmingly cited as being well
   groomed. Women thought of themselves as poised; men saw
   them as well dressed. Investigation should substantiate the
   fact that professional women tend to be as well groomed as
   the men.

It would appear that the professional woman is reacting to
stereotypes of herself rather than to real differences in qualifications, and she reflects this stereotyped image even more
strongly than does the man. There is a cultural lag between her
achievements and the development of appropriate attitudes to
support those achievements. Professional women are apparently attempting *identification* with a stereotyped role rather
than searching for *identity* as persons.

This is to be expected. The overriding aim of education for
women in the United States has been to make it as good as that
for men. The dominant fact of life for women is that society
thereupon makes different demands and no longer cares what
women do with the education they have received. But attitudes
are absorbed along with knowledge and facts. Unused talents,
unrelated tasks and discrepancy between effort and reward remain to plague the working woman, whether she is married or
single. The multiplicity of roles, so often described as peculiar
to women, boils down to a single role, that of homemaker, and
the "either-or" proposition, persistent and all-powerful, stands
between the woman and the professional role with which she
is trying to identify. This is a false issue. The woman who has
a profession but no husband or children nevertheless continues

to feel somewhat less than a woman. And the woman who has both husband and children but no profession continues to feel somewhat less than a person. The problem for women is to have a clearer image of themselves, of their needs and goals as individuals, so that they can distinguish between themselves as "personalities" and their requirements as professionals. Then, perhaps, like Alice in Wonderland, each will be able to decide where—ultimately—she really wants to get to.

Conventional patterns identify the man as provider and the woman as homemaker. When these lines blur, a period of readjustment is required until the cultural transition is completed. Such a transition is now going on. Times have changed but the image of the roles of men and women have not kept pace even among those whose education has kept them up-to-date with new ideas. Do we, as a recent massive survey suggests, still need to know more about the differences between men and women, more about the nature of women's emotional responses, more about women's capacity to learn, and more about the pattern of women's lives? The important fact we need to know is that we are not acting upon the facts we have, but rather, we continue to act on the stereotypes which available facts have, in numerous instances, already disproved. The best minds of those persons most dedicated to the problems of the woman are held, almost by hypnotic compulsion, to a re-search for facts already known.

Dr. Patricia Sexton, authority on the working woman, keynotes the real problem of the professional woman when she said in a letter to me:

Like all working women, she is a member of a de facto minority group in the working world. Only the professional woman is, if anything, more marginal to her occupation, more discriminated against, more ambivalent about her professional and private lives, and, paradoxically (in view of her generally high levels of awareness), perhaps less aware of minority group status than most other working women.

In contradictory fashion, it would appear that the professional woman, while least aware of her minority group status, is still among the most sensitive to that status. Like all minority groups she seems to accept the stereotype and, in a sense, reinforce it.

Looking at the problem from a cross-cultural perspective, scientific findings have shown that sex differences in working capabilities do not hold true universally; instead, they are culturally determined. The capabilities of women have been shown over and over again to be, in both "primitive" and urban societies, exactly what each society says they are. One need only look at the Russian woman today and the wide variety of work she is performing to realize that cultural motivation and cultural orientation are what actually account for what a woman can and does accomplish. Yet, even in the face of this evidence college educated women in the United States continue to constitute what Mary Bunting, president of Radcliffe College, recently called "our greatest waste of talent." [4] In the second half of the twentieth century this problem concerns more than the professional woman as an individual—it concerns the very welfare of the nation. "We do not know if women scientists are as competent as men," Dr. Bunting continues. "We do not know simply because we've never bothered to find out. But it doesn't matter. We need all kinds of people today, not just the physicist who sends off the satellite. Of all the talented people who don't go to college the majority are women." [5]

The problem of wasted female talent requires a great variety of answers, for the issue at stake is the maximum realization of individual potentiality. There are, however, many fields opening up in which women can function with a great deal of ease.

New Fields. Anthropology is an example of a new field in

[4] Mary Bunting, "Our Greatest Waste of Talent Is Women" (New York, *Life Magazine,* January 13, 1961).
[5] *Ibid.*

which women have participated. Indeed, I am frequently asked, "Why are there so many women anthropologists?" Three factors have operated to make this possible: (1) as a new behavioral science women, like other minorities, entered, set a high standard and kept the doors open for other women as the field expanded; (2) these pioneer women were imaginative enough to accept themselves as professionals; and (3) to encourage others, without regard for sex labels, to make anthropology their careers.

What has been true of anthropology is also true of other newer and expanding fields. We know that the sex labels attached to particular professions vary from society to society; they are different within the subgroups of the same society; they are different at different moments of history within the same society. There is always a period in a new occupation or in expanding areas of an old profession when sex labels are only loosely affixed because the primary need is for proper skills to perform a specific function. Rarely have so many new fields opened up as are now opening in the United States. Women can and must examine them.

Expanding Fields. As a culture develops it inevitably places stress on different kinds of professional skills. Currently, we in the United States are aware of this generalization as we face shortages in areas which were once well populated with qualified personnel. New attitudes toward health, toward science, toward intellectualism, are pressuring the teaching, social work and health fields.

These are traditional fields for women in which they have a backlog of experience. Even though more and more men enter the competition, expanding horizons demand that the very base of administration and leadership be broadened to utilize the full potential of those who have long been prepared. This is possible, however, only if women who have been traditionally involved can grasp the new ideas and, with pioneering skill, begin to seek answers to new questions.

When a profession expands in relation to the demands society makes upon it there are new problems which cannot be answered by stereotyped solutions; but a sense of the past is needed to find the most appropriate and longterm answers.

Established Fields. In many long-established fields, the limited access of women to top-level positions, their inability to progress upward along the same well-defined routes as those established for men, clearly results in a loss of potential talent. It is in those occupations in which the numerical proportion of men to women is most equal, as in the business world, that a' dual progress plan functions. Women enter as typists and move up a promotional escalator quite different from the one men are on; it is an escalator that does not allow women to compete with men. If women are to avoid being placed on a distinctly feminine and stereotyped promotion schedule, they must carefully consider their own aspirations in relation to such patterns. If they hope to attain a professional status, women must choose to forgo early satisfactions of money, personal-helper status and prestige, and enter the professional escalator in competition with men.

For those women who, because of personal needs or aspirations—usually in the wife-and-mother role—get started on the clerical escalator in spite of previous professional training, this pattern in our achievement-oriented society may not be possible. They must look squarely at their own problems and desires. It is not impossible for women to utilize their professional training, even if they remain technically in the clerical classification. But it is difficult without sustained professional contacts.

For the professional businesswoman, painter, musician, editor, who is also a mother, the problems are quite real and quite serious. She, unlike the single woman or the part-time professional, needs to face the question of whether or not she can play the typical mother role. Her relationships with her children and husband can be positive and warm, but she can never create the child-centered family which has come to be the ideal today. She can be worried about her children, but the show must go on. This means that both she and her children have to learn somehow—and very early—to accept her professional status.

These dual satisfactions of wife and career woman are not, however, for every woman. This, too, professional women must face honestly. The role of the professional woman in meeting her problems demands: 1. That she help stop the decrease in the proportion of women in the professions by not avoiding those careers labeled "for men only." If she does shun "men only" professions she is her own worst enemy, not only because she may fail to assess her own fitness and qualifications, but because she consciously or unconsciously tends to counsel younger women away from men's occupations. 2. That she play an active role in endeavors aimed at increasing her personal and material satisfactions so that they are fairly equivalent with those accorded other working women. She must stop accepting the lower status and the lower salary simply because she is a woman. 3. That she accept the fact that she is apt to play multiple and often contradictory roles. Rather than regard this state as *abnormal* she ought to regard it as *normal,* thus minimizing the anxieties and tensions currently bedeviling her. Men, too, play multiple roles. There is just less talk and public frustration about them. 4. That she repudiate the false image she herself creates by searching for personal identity based upon reality rather than identification with an old stereotype. 5. And last, that she learn that the qualities of leadership and followership, of intellectual curiosity, of emotional stability, are not the exclusive prerogatives of any one sex or group but, rather, in combination they are the hallmark of the mature person.

Perhaps this is the way that professional women *ought to walk from here.*

WOMEN IN INDUSTRY

Lillian M. Gilbreth

Lillian M. Gilbreth, President of Gilbreth Inc., Consulting Engineers in Management, received her B.Litt. and her M.Litt. from the University of California, and her Ph.D. from Brown University. She is the widow of Frank Bunker Gilbreth who was a pioneer in industrial management; she is an authority on management in her own right and has published several books on management in industry and in the home. She is the mother of twelve children, two of whom immortalized the Gilbreth family in the famous biography, *Cheaper by the Dozen*.

In this country scientific management began with the engineering group. At that time, and during the early years of its development, those who were active in the movement were men. They were mechanical engineers, using the techniques and human relations practices typical of the engineer of that time. It is clear, as we read the articles written by these pioneers, that they had a deep concern for what happened to people. You will find this in *The Golden Book of Management*,[1] edited by Col. Lyndell Urwick, as he refers to the proceedings of the American Society of Mechanical Engineers, and also in *Classics in Management*,[2] edited by Harwood Merrill.

In the pioneers' day neither engineers nor anyone else for that matter had access to the material on human relations in industry that is available today. At that time it was nonexistent. Psychology was largely experimental, concerned with tests, the learning process and similar topics; sociology was barely devel-

[1] London, Newman Neame Ltd., 1956.
[2] New York, American Management Association.

oping; psychiatry was well on its way, but had not yet simplified its vocabulary to the point at which industrial engineers
could readily understand what was available from that source.

The important things in scientific management, then as
now, were, first, the code of ethics to which the pioneers con-
formed and, second, the methods they used to develop their
work in the industrial field. The code is simply stated: "To utilize the resources of nature and of human nature for the
benefit of mankind." The method was typically scientific—the
questioning method. As the questions were carefully put and
carefully answered it became clear that problems fell into two
broad classifications—the development of natural resources and
the development of human resources. Obviously, human resources include women as well as men, and it was recognized
that the development of the feminine segment of our human
resources was of tremendous importance.

It is interesting to note that among the writers in the
pioneer group one woman is included in *The Golden Book of
Management*. She is Mary Parker Follett, a sociologist and a social worker, who had deep regard for the importance of what
was happening in industry. It is interesting, too, that in her
writings she did not stress the problems of women, but took it
for granted that industry must concern itself with all people in
that field. A careful reading of what she said shows that the
techniques which she developed and the attitudes on which
they were built, were not only effective at the time they were
created but are as good today—and likely to be as good through
the future—as they were in the beginning. She recognizes that
people need to communicate easily and participate wholeheart-
edly, and that everyone who takes part in a project should feel
he has something worthwhile to contribute and that the results
will include his contribution.

There were other women of this same period who bore the
needs of women constantly in mind. While they would not perhaps be classified as management people, they were active in the

industrial field. Take for example, the Goldmark sisters—Josephine and Pauline. They were the sisters-in-law of Louis Bran-
deis, who contributed so generously to the development of scientific management. They both had industrial experience and
their book on fatigue is as interesting and stimulating today as
it was when it was written.

Early in the development of scientific management the
government also turned its attention to problems affecting
women. The Labor Department established a special Women's
Bureau. While some felt that perhaps women were over protected in requirements for health, welfare and safety, and that
not enough time was spent on vigorous campaigning for equality of women with men, the Women's Bureau was fortunate in
having at its head Mary Anderson—a woman who had had experience herself as a worker in industry, and who continued to
keep closely in touch with women on the job, with their activities, their skills and the satisfactions the jobs offered.

It may be useful to think about some of the areas in which
scientific management has penetrated, to see how it has affected
opportunities and responsibilities for women in industry, and
to examine, by way of contrast, the problems which have developed in countries that are still without adequate means of sci-
entifically appraising industry.

At the first International Congress for Scientific Management, held in Prague in 1924, the program covered practically
every field of interest. No program since that time has been
quite so universal. The discussions covered not only what happened in factories and in offices but what took place on farms,
in homes, in the government and, in fact, in every area in which
work goes on.

The congress was sponsored by both the government of
Czechoslovakia and the Academy Masaryk, a scientific institution for research with a broad approach to subjects considered
and to methods of consideration, so it was quite natural that it
should furnish a forum for many kinds of activity. The delegates

from America, mostly members of the American Society of Mechanical Engineers, participated in the organization of the congress. In fact, my husband spent the preceding February as a guest of the Czech government, helping in the congress organization. The Management Committee of the ASME worked with the Czech group in organizing the congress, and many of its members gave papers and participated in the discussion. Upon request they also demonstrated the way in which such conferences would be conducted in the United States. The sessions were supplemented by visits to the industrial plants of Czechoslovakia and by trips through the beautiful countryside.

Having participated in these visits, and having spent some time at the Bata shoe factory as guest of the wife of the owner, I was able to see for myself the way in which American ideas on the technical aspects of factory organization and operation had been adopted. I observed the care with which women were safeguarded on their jobs and the interesting assignments in which many of them were engaged. I could also observe the way in which the wife of the owner and wives of the other executives participated in making membership in the organization satisfying from the human relations standpoint—in the factory, the office, the sales division and as overseas representatives.

The part that women play in the congresses is important. There were a number of activities planned for women who did not care to attend the technical meetings. Most women attended the formal opening and closing sessions which were devoted to general problems of management. In addition, a great many took part in the workshops at which papers were presented and discussed, and they went on the excursions to industrial plants included in the technical program.

There were two "Women's Sessions," one in Sydney and one in Melbourne, which attracted large audiences of women and a number of men. It was interesting to see the men's reaction to the case material presented. This case material was definitely the firsthand experience of women who had tried and succeeded in carrying management into their activities. At one of the panels four women spoke.

The representative from England has a husband and three children and a very rich and rewarding family life. She is also a topflight consultant, heading her own large organization, in which there are many men. What she said was impressive indeed, and those of us who knew her felt that she could not pos-sibly have overstated the satisfaction which carrying out her life project has brought to her family and co-workers.

Another woman came from Hong Kong. She had had professional training, but when she married she prepared to devote herself to home and family—only to find that tradition dictated that the mother-in-law should supervise and manage this area. Therefore, to everybody's satisfaction, she went back to her own work, adapting her program to conform to the traditional family setup of the country.

Still another came from the Philippines. She had not had a technical background or experience but had great ability and an interest in a career and in volunteer work as well. When she found that, as a married woman with adequate help and rela-tives nearby, she had time to spare, she went to the nearest barrio and became interested in arts and crafts and helped the women there set up a program and find a market.

The fourth woman, an Australian, said that she had found her home and family a full-time job, but discovered as time went on that volunteer experiences outside the home made family life itself richer and more rewarding. So she herself participated and helped other members of her family to get the necessary train-ing and education to work in this field. These are four very dif-ferent ways in which women can make a contribution to society while discharging fully and satisfactorily their traditional obli-gations and responsibilities.

While the subjects discussed at the congresses have changed with time, the member countries of the international group have organized a congress every three years in peacetime and have continued a balanced presentation of both technical and human relations problems, including those which uniquely affect women.

It is not possible in a chapter of this length to trace this development through the various congresses. However, the Twelfth Congress, held in Australia in 1960, showed very clearly that scientific management was of interest and was attempted in many countries including those which have only recently gained autonomy.

To take the measure of a problem, management asks six questions. *What* is being done? *Who* is doing it? *Where* is it being done? *When* is it being done? *Why* is it being done? *How* is it being done? These questions, fully answered, give us the information we need. Of particular importance are the *how* and the *why*. *How* leads to a consideration of the skills necessary for doing work, ways in which work can be simplified and the satisfactions which can result. Thus it explores both the technical and the human relations aspects of work.

Pearl Franklin Clark, in her *Challenge of the American Know-How*,[3] sets forth the ideals back of this work and relates the experience of our men and women who have gone, in war and in peace, to work in other countries. The book demonstrates that training in the American know-how has led to both a willingness to attack problems and a capacity to transfer skill from one work area to another and use it effectively.

The question *why* has led to a new and growing emphasis on human relations. As a result, an interdisciplinary group, with representatives from the fields of psychology, sociology, psychiatry and other related sciences, is today working closely with our men of technical background in recognition of the fact that management is an art as well as a science.

All this may seem, at first glance, to be widely removed from the problems of women in industry. However, this is not the case. I find it helpful, in discussing the scope of manage-

[3] New York, Hillary House, 1948, 1957.

ment, to consider the five areas in personal life in which management can be profitably applied.

First, we have the problem of managing ourselves—all too
often a sadly neglected task. As we grow up we must learn to
know ourselves, to handle our emotional drives constructively,
to accept responsibility and be able to cooperate with other
people.

If we are fortunate, many of these lessons are learned at
home as children, for the home and family life is the second
area in which good management plays a vital role. As we grow
up we all need a place in which we can safely experiment, make
a few trial flights and learn how to handle simple problems before we are faced with the greater complexity of the grown-up
world.

Generally speaking, the homemaking practices of the
present generation offer unusually fine opportunities for this
type of training. In today's usually servantless homes family
teamwork has become the accepted way of life. Housekeeping
tasks are no longer the sole responsibility of the wife and mother,
for husband and children share the work in order that mother
may share the recreation which follows. The old sharp line of
distinction between woman's work and man's work in the home
is fast melting away.

The status of women employed to help in the home has
changed enormously with the years. I can well remember the
women who helped in our household when I was growing up,
and I remember the work they did and the long hours they labored. Often they came from other countries; usually they "lived
in" and their housing and privileges were universally restricted.
I can remember with amusement the shock it was to the ladies
of my mother's generation when I said that I hoped to live to
see the day when every domestic servant would live in her own
home, and be able to ask and get adequate wages, good working
hours and a choice of other occupations if she had the capacity

and the wish for it. If we check what has happened in this field I feel sure we shall be encouraged.

In the third area, volunteer work, which offers such diverse opportunities and responsibilities, the value of women's contribution can hardly be overestimated. Anyone who has participated in volunteer activities realizes that without this kind of help most of the health, welfare and education institutions in this country would come to a standstill.

The same thing is true in civic activities. We have, for example, the work of the League of Women Voters, and of the women who have gone into national, state and local government, into our foreign service and the armed forces. All of these activities are vital to our national welfare.

As for career jobs, these are increasing daily in variety, in scope and in interest, and they are being nurtured by the women's organizations. The American Association of University Women, the Women Deans and Counselors, the Business and Professional Women, the Personnel Women, can all take pride in the creditable work they are doing.

The Society of Women Engineers is an example of what women have done in the engineering profession. Opportunities for training in engineering have always been available to women in the land-grant colleges, and the engineering departments of many other colleges and universities have been willing to accept carefully selected women students.

Through self-discipline and hard work, the fine young women of this small group prepared to take their place in industry but found that placement was not easy. It was years before the industrial scouts who came to the universities in search of personnel were willing to interview women students on the same terms as men. However, those who were given an opportunity did well. During wartime, of course, placement was easier. The real hurdle, as it is for pioneer women in so many professions, proved to be advancement.

The Society of Women Engineers, with members all over the United States, has done much to help its members achieve status in their profession. Qualifications for membership include a degree from an accredited university, activity in an appropriate branch of engineering and membership in an engineering organization. The society has established an office in the United Engineering Center and its members participate in the responsibilities, as well as the privileges, which the building has to offer.

The high caliber of programs, publications and plans for the future all indicate the technical adequacy of the society. The fine fellowship which has developed within the society, and with other engineering groups, testifies to the human relations side.

Scientific management has much to offer women in every facet of their lives. Techniques which were originally developed for use in industry have since been successfully applied to every field of human endeavor as well as to the direction of individual lives. To those who are interested in the status of women in the future I would say: evaluate the management opportunities being offered in all kinds of undertakings and in all countries, and see which ones can be usefully applied to the problems which face women. Try to discover their similarities, often hidden at first glance by surface differences; apply the questioning method until the problem is clearly and accurately defined; then use the time-tested techniques which scientific management places at your disposal.

If we pursue this course with vigor, with interest and with enthusiasm, we should be able to meet our future responsibilities with complete satisfaction.

GIFTED WOMEN IN THE TRADE UNIONS

Bessie Hillman

Bessie Hillman is vice-president of the Amalgamated Clothing Workers Union, mother of two and grandmother of four. She is active in the fields of civil rights, education and child welfare. She is a member of the Civil Rights Committee of the National AFL-CIO, a member of the American Association for the United Nations and of the American Labor Education Service.

In 1960, an estimated 23 million women were employed in business and industry in the United States, comprising about one-third of the total labor force. This was an alltime high, far exceeding even the World War II years, when so many millions of women who never dreamed of working again outside their own homes suddenly found themselves manning assembly lines and vast office installations.

Of these 23 million, almost 3½ million are members of labor unions, comprising about 19 per cent of all union members and 15 per cent of all women in the labor force. Yet only two of 184 international trade unions (listed in the 1959 directory of unions issued by the United States Labor Department) had women presidents, and both of these were tiny unions in the entertainment field. Four had women in the office of secretary-treasurer—again all relatively small organizations with a very high proportion of women members. Not one of the fifty AFL-CIO state central bodies is headed by a woman, and only one has a woman secretary-treasurer. Of the hundreds of city and county central bodies of labor, although a completely up-to-date roster is not available, it is safe to say that not more than perhaps half a dozen have any full-time paid women executive officers.

While there are several dozen women among the thousands of vice-presidents of international unions, nearly all of them come from unions with predominantly female membership, e.g., teaching, office employment, retail sales, men's and woman's clothing manufacture. But even in these, the number of women officers in relation to female membership is minute. For example, the major unions in the women's and men's wear industries—each with between 70 and 80 per cent women in a combined total membership of over 800,000—have one and three women respectively on their twenty-odd-member general executive boards. Moreover, only a minority of the handful of women vice-presidents hold full-time paid posts in their internationals and fewer still are in a position to decisively influence policy even in their own unions, much less in the labor movement as a whole.

At a recent AFL-CIO national convention, only 23 of the approximately 900 accredited delegates were women—all of them, of course, top officers of their respective international or local organizations. The memberships represented by these 900 delegates included almost three million women out of a grand total of about 13½ million AFL-CIO members. Frequently, a union is not entitled to as many delegates as it has general executive board members; in these cases it is generally the women board members who must be content with the position of alternate delegate.

Another striking commentary on the place accorded women in the labor movement can be found by examining the index of almost any volume of American labor history. In Philip Taft's massive and definitive two-volume history of the AFL, for example, just sixteen women appear among the thousands of index entries—and all but four of these are either foreign labor leaders or women whose names appear solely in the preface as having assisted the author in researching or editing.

Not surprisingly, many women in the labor movement accuse their male colleagues of deliberately and systematically barring them from positions of top leadersihp. There have been instances in which male members of a union executive body have quite obviously opposed the leadership aspirations of a woman member despite her unquestioned competence. But whether it is a case of deliberate intent or, as would appear to be the general rule, merely a combination of male intransigence or prejudice, female apathy or resignation, and the all-encompassing mire of tradition, the plain fact is that women are not playing their proper role of leadership in the American labor movement.

Of course there are hundreds of women in various paid or volunteer posts within international, state or local labor bodies, and many of them are doing outstanding jobs and are among the most highly respected individuals in their fields, but nearly all of them are in the third or fourth—or lower—echelon of union leadership; few are in a position to help set policy or to significantly influence the direction the trade union movement takes.

These statistics have been cited, of course, in order to suggest the vast leadership possibilities in the labor movement for capable women. I am not referring now to positions such as shop stewards or local union officers, in which thousands of women now serve faithfully and competently. In eliminating this group of women from consideration here, I am not in any sense downgrading their value to the labor movement and to the society in which they function. Indeed, in concert with their male counterparts, with whom they work harmoniously and almost without exception on an equal footing, these women form the backbone of the labor movement and a pillar of our economic structure. Without their support, the top leadership of labor would be unable to function.

Since there is no dearth of published material on how these women serve—and are served by—the trade union movement, I shall confine myself to a discussion of the opportunities and responsibilities at the executive level which women can and should find in the American labor movement.

First, in all fairness, it must be observed that the early history of the trade unions in America (and by "early" history I mean only as far back as the late nineteenth and early twentieth centuries, when unions first began to emerge as a force to be reckoned with on the national scene) does evidence the contributions of some outstanding women—though even here, while their influence was often great, few attained positions of top official leadership. The legendary figure of Mary Jones (known to all her contemporaries as Mother Jones) will never fade from the labor history books. Of all the women who have led labor in America, she is the one whose role seems most closely to have paralleled that traditionally assigned to men. For over half a century (from 1871 when she joined the old Knights of Labor almost until her death in 1930 at the age of 100), this dauntless and literally indestructible woman marched up and down the country organizing mine workers and other exploited toilers. Her heroism and devotion in the face of great hardship and often grave personal danger have marked her as a sort of Joan of Arc of the labor movement.

Another inspired—and almost unsung—pioneer of labor was Clara Lemlich, who sparked the organizing struggles of the waist workers in the early 1900s.

Of the other movers and shakers of labor among women, most were identified in one way or another with either the National Women's Trade Union League—that extraordinary body of women that originated in Great Britain and established itself here in the first years of this century; or with Hull House, the pioneer settlement house in Chicago that played so large a part in the early organizing drives in that area.[1]

Still, it must be recorded that, unlike Mother Jones and

[1] The list of leaders of these two organizations is a roll of honor for women unionists: Jane Addams, not only one of the greatest women but one of the greatest human beings this country has ever produced; Margaret Drier Robins; Agnes Nestor; Sophonisba Breckinridge; Rose Schneiderman; Mary Anderson; Elizabeth Christman; Alice Henry; Ellen Gates Starr; Mary McDowell; Grace and Edith Abbott; Florence Kelley; Mary Drier; Ethel Smith; Lillian Wald; Cornelia Bryce Pinchot and many others.

Clara Lemlich, most of these women did not come from the ranks of working women, but were educators, social workers, writers and editors, and even wealthy society matrons with a social conscience, who fought for the rights and welfare of the exploited and the underprivileged. What distinguishes them from the thousands of well-meaning and even well-doing women from different social strata who have defended the rights of the workers is that these women actively *organized,* and most of them did not hesitate to walk a picket line, address a strike meeting or angrily harangue an employer or a hostile government official. In short, they did more than merely encourage the early trade union struggles; they became part of them.

Another group of women identified with labor, many of them still active, came from the early workers' education efforts such as the Bryn Mawr and Hudson Shore Summer schools, Brookwood Labor College, the Southern Workers School and the Workers' Education Bureau.[2] Again, few of these were ever actually "working girls" in the accepted sense, but they came to be identified with the labor movement through a deep and abiding devotion to the welfare and progress of those who toil with their hands.

Some women have managed to draw a bit closer to the inner councils of labor. Many of them are still active, others only recently departed.[3]

[2] This group includes Hilda Smith, first director of the Bryn Mawr and Hudson Shore schools; Frieda Miller, who went on to become New York State industrial commissioner and later director of the Women's Bureau of the U.S. Department of Labor; Eleanor Coit, now director of the American Labor Education Service; Alice Hanson Cook, a former union education director, now a professor at the New York State School of Industrial & Labor Relations; Dorothy Oko, director of labor education services for the New York Public Library; Orlie Pell, Brownie Lee Jones, Mildred Tompkins and a number of others.

[3] For instance, Esther Peterson, firebrand legislative representative of the AFL-CIO's Industrial Union Department; Josephine Roche, director of the United Mine Workers' Welfare & Retirement Fund; Caroline Davis, director of women's activities for the United Auto Workers; Margaret Thornburgh and Esther Murray, co-directors of the Women's Activities Division of the AFL-CIO Committee on Political Education; Jennie Matyas, San Francisco education

Impressive as are the achievements of all of these women, it will be noted that the highest rank attained by any of them *within* the labor movement is that of vice-president of an international union. While many international vice-presidents exercise considerable influence, not only in their own particular unions but sometimes in the highest councils of the labor movement, it must be pointed out that this is more often attributable to their own personal gifts or prestige than to any authority inherent in the office of vice-president. It is a well-known fact that most unions, like their opposite numbers in the business world, like to have a generous array of vice-presidents (from ten to as many as thirty is the general rule) as a matter either of recognition for past service or of geographical representation or both.

On the other hand, some of the most able and influential of these women operate in key staff positions. Esther Peterson, Josephine Roche and Pauline Newman are excellent examples. Still, they are seldom in a position to *create* policy, capable as they may be of interpreting or carrying it out.

In another category are the leaders of the various auxiliary bodies. These include, first of all, the special departments within the labor movement set aside for "women's activities," like the women's divisions of COPE and of the UAW which have already been mentioned. They are set up to serve the special requirements and interests of women workers within their particular jurisdictions—and many people feel that they are rapidly becoming an anachronism as the status of rank-and-file women workers approaches equality with that of men.

---

director and former vice-president of the International Ladies Garment Workers Union; Pauline Newman, veteran education director of the ILGWU health center in New York; Rose Pesotta, former vice-president and colorful leader of the ILGWU, who has written several books on labor; Gladys Dickason, vice-president and former research director for the Amalgamated Clothing Workers; the late Dorothy Jacobs Bellanca, vice-president and dedicated organizer for the Amalgamated Clothing Workers who became known as the Joan of Arc of the ACW; Selma Borchardt, seasoned Washington representative for the American Federation of Teachers; Marie Downey and Marie Caylor, editors respectively of the Brotherhood of Electrical Workers' and the Federation of Teachers' prize-winning official publications.

Then we have the women who lead the various groups which are in the nature of appendages to the body of labor. These are the so-called "ladies' auxiliaries," organized primarily to enlist the interest and support of wives, sisters and other female relatives of active male union members. Their day-to-day activities are more social than organizational or political, and they are not on the whole held in the highest esteem by the more sophisticated among labor leaders.

Finally, there are a number of bodies set up to serve women workers but which are not an integral part of the labor movement. One of these is the Women's Bureau of the Department of Labor, established in 1918 to promote the special concerns of women workers. Mary Anderson was its first and longtime director, appointed by President Wilson and reappointed by succeeding presidents until her retirement in 1944. President Truman named Frieda Miller to the post, and Alice K. Leopold served under President Eisenhower. (It will be remembered, of course, that Frances Perkins was a distinguished Secretary of Labor throughout the administration of Franklin D. Roosevelt—the first and so far only woman Cabinet member. With Miss Perkins as Secretary and Miss Miller as Women's Bureau director, the Labor Department in those years was indeed a fountainhead of progress and reform in matters affecting women workers!)

The National Women's Trade Union League, which functioned from 1903 until 1955, when it disbanded, was an outstanding example of a non-governmental body dedicated to promoting the welfare not only of women but of all workers. At its first national convention in 1907 the league elected Margaret Drier Robins as president. She provided inspired leadership until her retirement in 1922, when she was succeeded by Maud Swartz. Rose Schneiderman became president in 1926, and held the post throughout the rest of the league's active existence until her widely lamented retirement in 1947. Elizabeth Christman was secretary from 1921 until the organization disbanded, and it is her name which has come to be most closely identified with its history in more recent years. Though the league, as an organization, no longer exists, the NWTUL name still does—as sponsor of annual college scholarships for women with an interest in trade unions or the social services.

At its peak the NWTUL numbered more than one million members, mostly women but also many men who were in accord with its aims, chief of which was to educate women on the advantages of trade union membership. But it was also a dynamic social force for progress and reform in many areas, as well as a sort of national clearinghouse for information on labor matters. In the years since its suspension, some of its labor functions have been carried on, more or less perfunctorily, by organizations whose primary concerns lie elsewhere, e.g., the Women's International League for Peace & Freedom and the League of Women Voters.

An organization which functions within the entire labor movement, but which has perhaps a somewhat larger impact on women workers, is the American Labor Education Service, headed by Eleanor Coit. Its principal activity is setting up and conducting educational institutes and seminars for union members. Though it operates independently of the labor movement, it considers itself responsible to labor. It is largely supported through contributions and grants by labor organizations, and many union officials serve on its board of directors. Among women who are or have been assosiated with the ALES, besides Miss Coit, are Orlie Pell, Theresa Wolfson, Fannie Turkel, Brownie Lee Jones, Eleanor Anderson and Marie Algor.

So much for a brief—and very superficial—review of the past and present performance of women in the trade union movement. Now let us return to our principal theme: How can the woman of talent and imagination contribute to the advancement of her working sisters in the immediate future?

I have pointed out the insignificant role played by women in the top councils of the movement. It would be unrealistic to suggest that any contemporary woman now outside the house of labor (unless she is very young, with a career still to be chosen) should aspire, say, to the presidency or secretary-treasurership of a major labor federation or international union. Unlike many business organizations, one thing that can be said for most labor unions is that they have a tradition of promoting from within, and by and large, on the basis of contributions made by their staffs. Chances are that the men (or women) who will become the presidents or other top officials of virtually every major union on the American scene during the next twenty or so years are already on the staffs of their respective unions, or at least working in the trade or industry. Perhaps this suggests an undesirable tendency toward inbreeding or parochialism, but on the other hand it squares with the basic union concept that a man has a right to advancement based on a combination of seniority and ability. Trade unionists generally resent rank outsiders (with or without nepotism or other favoritism) who ride in over the heads of workers who have given their best years in the service of an organization.

So the day when substantial numbers of women will occupy their rightful places as presidents or other executive officers of unions must await another generation (today's high school and college girls now pondering careers please note!). It is in the area of professional staff positions, both inside and on the periphery of the movement, that the major opportunities lie. Here, few unions and certainly none of the important service organizations, have any compunctions about bringing in outside people who they are convinced would promote their objectives. And while prejudice against women, even in some staff positions, still exists in a few labor bodies, it is gradually being overcome. Qualified women may feel reasonably confident that their applications will receive equal consideration with those of men.

It may sound old-fashioned and even biased, but I have a

deep conviction that, given a more important function within
the labor movement, women could do much to restore the union
image as the indomitable fighter for social justice and enlighten-
ment, an image that has been sadly undermined in recent years.
This is particularly true in workers' education and community
relations, fields in which women have traditionally played a
rather larger part than they have in the organizational structure
of the movement (witness Jane Addams, Margaret Robins,
Eleanor Coit and others already mentioned).

Nearly all major international unions today have their own
education departments, which keep a constant stream of pamphlets, reports and other informational materials going out to
their various constituent bodies and which organize frequent
institutes, seminars, tours and other educational activities. Most
of these education departments work closely with universities in
their respective areas and with cooperating agencies such as the
American Labor Education Service, and they generally coordi-
nate their programs with the education department of the
national AFL-CIO in Washington.

In addition to the international unions, more and more
state federations and even major city central bodies are coming
to recognize the value of organized educational activities. Some
of the larger organizations have already established their own
education departments, and almost all of them work, to a greater
or lesser degree, with institutions of learning in the locality.

While almost all major universities offer some adult or
workers' education courses, a few are particularly noted for
their comprehensive programs in labor education and industrial
relations. These include the New York State School of Industrial & Labor Relations, an adjunct of Cornel University; Rut-
gers University in New Jersey; the University of Wisconsin's
School for Workers; Pennsylvania State University; the joint
program of the University of Michigan, Michigan State University and Wayne State University; the University of California

at Berkeley; Illinois University; Minnesota University; Chicago University and Roosevelt University.[4]

Apart from teaching itself, there are opportunities for women in administrative and liaison positions in this growing complex of union-educational institution cooperation: Women of vigor and ideas can do much to enlarge the scope and elevate the standards of this program which so far has only scratched the surface. What is especially needed is more emphasis on the humanities, politics and the broader cultural aspects of education for workers, as distinct from the organizational and "tool" subjects such as parliamentary procedure, public speaking, etc., which receive the lion's share of attention now. In this regard, much can be learned from a study of workers' education programs in England and the Scandinavian countries.

Another area to which the trained or gifted woman can contribute is economic and social research. With the increasing complexity of industrial relations, unions have found that self-contained research facilities are an absolute essential if the union is to service its members properly and maintain its place as a factor in its particular industry. Almost every major international union has its own research department, which usually incorporates the union's often extensive library and sometimes is combined with the education department into an education-research arm. State federations and larger city central bodies are also becoming aware of the need for research departments— again often combined with respectable libraries and education activities.

Few union research departments are now headed by women, though many women act as associates or staff specialists. There is room for many more women all along the line. It is hardly necessary to add that library service has traditionally been

[4] A unique school, maintained by the International Ladies Garment Workers Union, offers a practical one-year course, combining both class instruction and on-the-job training, in all aspects of union leadership. Applicants need not have college degrees, and employment with the ILGWU is guaranteed to those who satisfactorily complete the course.

the province of women. While not too many unions have as yet felt the need to employ a full-time trained librarian, the trend certainly is in that direction.

Another field requiring professional staff is the publications or public relations department. Nearly every international union—certainly all the major ones—publishes a regular newspaper or magazine which automatically goes to each member, as well as to other unions, educational institutions, libraries, legislative and other government representatives, and interested individuals. Most state federations and many city bodies also have their own publications, and a large local union will almost certainly have a vehicle for regular communication with its members. Even many smaller locals go beyond a mere postcard notification of meetings or other functions, and will produce at least a monthly mimeographed newsletter.

Most of the more important labor journals—published weekly, semi-monthly or monthly—are professionally edited, and many compare favorably with the best of the smaller community newspapers or company house organs. (There are still a good number of labor newspapers which are privately owned and published, and merely "endorsed" or "sponsored" by an official labor organization, but they are generally frowned upon in the labor movement and their number is dwindling.)

The official union publication (a few unions have two or even three) is sometimes combined with a public relations or publicity department whose function is to issue general press releases on events in the union, help prepare speeches and articles for union officials and generally to keep the public informed of the union's role in public affairs through distribution of pamphlets and other materials.

While this is a limited and rather specialized field (few unions, even the largest, have a publications or public relations staff of more than three or four), it does offer possibilities for' women trained in journalism or promotional techniques. Marie Downey and Marie Caylor have already been mentioned as outstanding women labor editors in a field still overwhelmingly dominated by men.

I shall not dwell at length on the possibilities for women on the legal staffs of labor organizations, for the obvious reason that the law is one field in which women have always played a very small part. It would hardly be reasonable to suggest that they might shine in the realm of labor law when they have not done so in any other aspect of jurisprudence. Still, it should be noted that with the proliferation of labor laws, both federal and state, in the past decade and a half, labor organizations have expanded their legal staffs perhaps more rapidly than any other department in order to cope with the myriad problems posed by these mostly restrictive statutes. As the need for additional staff grows, women with a flair for the law might look into the possibilities. Trained legal secretaries, at any rate, are always in demand.

Administration of the vast welfare fund reserves being accumulated by unions, as well as financial administration of unions in general, call for skills which women are often well equipped to provide. In addition, the need for trained psychiatric social workers, to help union members who have emotional and family problems which may lead to alcoholism, absenteeism and job inefficiency, provides a new area of work for women in trade unions.

The activity most basic to labor unions remains to be discussed—organizing. Here it is not so much a matter of education or training, but rather of personality and native skills. Many of the most successful union organizers, both male and female, have been persons with little formal education and a minimum of vocational training. The one essential ingredient is ability to gain friends and supporters. Some training in public speaking and, of course, a basic orientation in union practices and procedures is usually necessary, but more important is a personality that can be both outgoing and aggressive and charismatically persuasive. A woman interested in entering this field must decide for herself whether she has or can cultivate these traits. At least in industries with substantial numbers of women workers, there would appear to be little prejudice against women as union organizers—if they can prove they have what it takes.

(It might be noted here that, while it is certainly the exception, there have been instances in which professional staff people have used these positions as steppingstones to top elective positions in unions. The position of organizer or business agent is of course the most logical one from which to step into an executive post.)

Lastly, and perhaps most important of all, there is the area of labor—community relations and services. In this field, women can render an important service to the labor movement and the community at once, serving, as it were, as a bridge or lifeline between the two. And, unlike the areas of union activity already outlined, there are opportunities here for a great deal of meaningful volunteer service for those willing and able to give it, as well as perhaps some full-time paid service.

As noted earlier, unions have become more and more aware of their community responsibilities, though few of them as yet play the pioneering social role that many of us feel they should. They have involved themselves in a wide range of community functions: United Fund campaigns, urban redevelopment planning, hospital and health drives, relief and rehabilitation efforts, library campaigns, blood banking, human relations and civic reform activities, and a host of other worthy causes. These demand vast amounts of time and energy—not to mention money —both within the labor organizations and in liaison areas. Fortunately, much of the time and energy can be contributed by volunteers, many of them, naturally enough, women.

Some of the ladies' auxiliaries of labor render valuable service to these functions. The national AFL-CIO has a community services department which offers guidance and coordination to local efforts; and state and local labor bodies are setting up community affairs committees. Many top union executives regularly and willingly take time off from busy schedules to participate in planning and carrying out community welfare and relief programs.

This will suggest how women with a sense of civic responsibility can be most helpful to *both* labor and the community. In offering their services, they will automatically be helping the community agencies concerned. But if at the same time they are genuinely devoted to labor's interests, they will, in the course of their community services, help to project on the community consciousness an image of labor that is more favorable than it has been in many instances in the past. They can also help to overcome, among their middle-class colleagues, whatever residue there may be of the oldtime tendency to disparage the "laboring classes."

The bulk of the paid professionals in these activities are, of course, employed by the service agencies themselves, rather than by supporting bodies such as labor unions. Still, in most communities there is a small number of full-time liaison positions in which labor organizations may pay all or part of the freight. These spots are usually filled by people with a labor background and some training or orientation in community service activities. In addition, there are a few paid professional positions within the community service departments of the national AFL-CIO and perhaps one or two other very large labor bodies. Women, by every standard of temperament and conditioning, would seem ideal for these jobs.

In volunteer efforts, much can be accomplished by women who can spare the necessary time and resources—and a full measure of devotion to the cause they seek to serve. The office of almost any state federation or major city central body should be able to furnish information on how would-be volunteers can serve. Or basic guidelines may be obtained by writing to the offices of the AFL-CIO Community Services Committee, 9 East 40th Street, New York City.

So far, this article has been addressed primarily to the ma-

ture woman, long finished with her formal education, perhaps
with school age or even grown children, who is considering entry or re-entry into some phase of professional activity or into
some socially useful occupation in which she can utilize special
experience or skills.

It must be recognized, of course, that if she is over forty or
forty-five, she will face, in addition to the normal problems of
job-hunting, the handicap of her age. This will be almost (though
perhaps not quite) as true in looking for a job in the labor field
as it is in private business. Everything else being equal, the
younger person, with a longer working life and development potential ahead of her, will have the inside track. But this does not
imply that the mature woman's plight is hopeless if she feels a
genuine urge to work in the labor movement. As of the present
moment, there is no oversupply of people of *any* age in *any* of
the specialized subdivisions of union activity discussed above.
Let no woman, therefore, who has set her heart on a labor career,
feel discouraged at least until she has given it a whirl.

At the risk of creating additional competition for the mature
woman, I feel this chapter would not be complete without a
word to her daughters and younger sisters.

Even among young men, let alone young women, those
who thoughtfully survey the occupational field and deliberately
and firmly choose a labor career are few and far between. Much
more often they come into it by accident or force of circum-
stance. Yet, for the socially oriented and capable young man *or*
woman, few fields offer greater spiritual, if not tangible, rewards.
The satisfaction that comes from knowing that one has improved the lot of one's fellows, not by charity or through a sense
of *noblesse oblige* but by helping them find the formula through
which they can help themselves, is hard to equal. The union
leader usually needs only to provide a spark; the rank and file
normally can be relied upon to catch fire and sweep forward under their own power and enthusiasm, often overtaking the
leader and pulling him along behind.

To the young woman now in high school or the early years of college, who is interested in the possibilities of a union career, here are a few suggestions: (1) plan to enroll in one of the schools of labor or industrial relations (several have already been listed, but there are others; your high school or college vocational adviser can put you on their track); (2) do not neglect your general education just because you have decided on a labor career. One of the most urgent needs today is labor leaders with a broader cultural background and keener awareness of social problems. Go just as far as you possibly can in the liberal arts or sciences—a college degree is important if not essential for most of the specialized union work described above; even a postgraduate degree will be no handicap; (3) read as widely and intensively as you can on not only labor but general social and economic problems. Read the biographies of some of the great labor leaders, and study some of their own writings; and (4) establish contacts with men and women functioning in union organizations and on the job in shop or factory. This will give you, at an early stage, some of the firsthand insights so essential to operating on your own.

Of course, helpful as they are, not every one of these steps is an absolute prerequisite to launching a union career. In the final analysis, whether you're twenty, thirty, forty or fifty, there is only one essential requirement (besides a reasonably high IQ and at least a nodding acquaintance with the English language): a sincere interest in the material well-being and the social, cultural and spiritual development of one's fellow human beings, together with a conviction that these goals can best be pursued by organization, education, and common dedication to a common cause.

This, after all, is what the labor movement stands for. And if it has not always lived up to its ideals, all the more reason for the intelligent, dedicated and socially motivated woman to come to its aid.

WOMEN IN EDUCATION

Vivian C. Mason

Vivian C. Mason received her Ph.B. from the University of Chicago. She is a well-known civic leader and former director of the Division of Social Service for the Department of Welfare of New York City. She also serves as education chairman of the Virginia State Conference of the NAACP, as chairman of the Norfolk Committee to Improve Public Education, and as a member of the Board of Directors of the Southern Regional Council. She was administrator of the "Temporary School for the Shutout Seventeen" and third president of the National Council of Negro Women.

For a considerable time, the United States enjoyed the distinction of being the only country in which a high school education is considered a right that is due every person, similar to the right to vote, to worship as one pleases or to express an unpopular opinion. We have always prided ourselves on our public school system, and teaching has been considered an important and honorable profession.

Women and education are almost synonomous. American women have always been in the forefront of the teaching profession, for teaching has been the best, most accessible avenue to economic and personal independence. For many years teaching carried a prestige rating which no other employment for women enjoyed, and it has always been regarded as a "respectable" vocation.

Unfortunately, however, for a variety of reasons, one of which is that the profession has been so largely dominated by women, the prestige accorded teachers has lost force and consistency. For the most part, this is a reflection of the value placed upon education by American citizens, and has little to do with the individual teacher—it encompasses the entire gamut of education. Our attitude is formed by non-educational factors like the allocation of taxes for educational facilities, the burgeoning of new communication media, the problems of people emerging from centuries of exploitation, the economic and social integration of large numbers of immigrants.

I suspect that part of the inanity that has afflicted the educational process stems from the fact that the majority of teachers have been women. This is not to imply that women have been lax in pushing ahead; to the contrary, they have exerted tremendous efforts to raise standards, to interest parents in education, and to project programs that will capture the imaginations of students who are sorely damaged by popular attitudes toward education.

The position of women in education by force of numbers is important. Eighty-eight per cent of all elementary school teachers and 54 per cent of all high school teachers are women; (only 20 per cent of college teachers are women!). They must exert much more force in the operation, administration and education of the general public as to conditions and goals of education. Moreover, their ideas must find political expression, for the public, perhaps because of its suspicion of our educational process, is asking questions about the kind of education American youth is receiving, the ends sought, how the image of America is projected and the breadth and depth of accomplishment after twelve years of formal education. Interest in the quality and content of the educational process has become a central concern for many organizations and individuals. Surveys and studies, promoted by the federal and state governments and by foundations and industries, are being conducted to secure facts and to interpret this body of material to the American public. Professional educators for many years have tested and experimented with all facets of education, striving to improve the process and to re-define methods and goals according to the needs of our times.

The phenomenal growth of the school population serves to re-emphasize the ills besetting the educational process. The first projections ever published of the level of education attained by the population of the United States were issued by the Bureau of the Census (series P-20 No. 91). In 1960, the report indicates, about 52 million students graduated from high school; a decade from then, 1970, the number will be 70 million, an increase of 18 million; and by 1980, the number will have reached 95 million. According to the projections, the percentage of the population of those aged 15 years and over who are high school graduates will rise from 35 per cent in 1950 to 55 per cent in 1980. Another result of the increase in mass schooling will be a sharp reduction in the number of people who have less than five years of formal education. It is also predicted that greater numbers of women will have completed high school than men, but more men than women are likely to receive college degrees.

There is, however, another side to this coin of education. While it appears that staggering numbers of young people graduate from high school each year, thousands fall by the wayside from the fifth grade on. These regiments of unknowns disappear in "do-not-know" statistics so dear to the charts of the poll-takers. The Educational Testing Service estimates that only 55 per cent of the pupils in the fifth grade will graduate from high school. From figures released by the United States Office of Education, *Today's Health* (April 1959) issued a warning—for the facts must be regarded as such—that in the average freshman class in high schools 25 per cent will drop out before graduation, and of those who reach the tenth grade 21 per cent will drop out before graduation. Other authorities estimate that over 35 per cent of potential graduates will not complete school. It follows, on the basis of approximate figures of 1,275,835 graduates in 1958, that more than 425,278 students were lost before graduation. They dropped out by the tenth grade and no resource was available to bring them back to the school community or to a logical point of achievement in their education.

The figures on dropouts in public schools and colleges obviously implies that serious, fresh and resourceful action by the school and community must be undertaken now. The ranks of the unemployed are swelled by these unskilled and unknown young people. They are a constant threat to wage standards, especially in sections of the country in which organized labor is weak, for unscrupulous employers welcome their cheap labor. A prey to vicious malpractices common in cities and smaller communities too, they are fresh fodder for criminal elements.

The reasons for these somewhat appalling figures cannot, of course, be laid at the doorstep of our school system alone, but our educational facilities are partly to blame, and it is quite clear that innovations and many drastic changes in the traditional administration of four-year high schools and colleges can be anticipated. Longer school hours, lengthened school terms, allocation of clerical work to clerical aides for teachers forecast even greater modifications in the future.

This is not enough. Alterations are also being made in the training of teachers, but in large part they have been hysterical responses to an increasingly tense world situation. A re-thinking of the role of the teacher and the ways in which he or she can most influence the students is demanded. Woman's cherishing role has many aspects, and teachers must assume that parents are giving the children the love and physical nourishment they require. It is the teacher's job—and this is the way in which she can be most effective—to stimulate her students to want to learn more; she must teach them facts, grammar and spelling and must introduce new ideas. She must, in brief, encourage them to love chemistry or mathematics or literature for the sake of the chemistry, mathematics and literature itself, and for the sake of increasing man's control over nature. We cannot afford to follow the tacit assumption our schools seem to be making that chemistry is not intrinsically interesting to youngsters. It is, and if the teacher thinks chemistry is interesting and important, the students will too.

We are overemphasizing the emotional aspects of the cherishing role and underemphasizing the intellectual. If teaching children arithmetic is not cherishing, well, then, this is where teaching departs from cherishing, but women are suited to do more than cherish children. The teachers we are turning out now are not sufficiently intelligent about scientific developments, about literary and artistic movements, and so on. They don't have the facts.

School administrators must also examine the opportunities given women to move up the promotion ladder. The opportunities for teachers in general are certainly expanding as the armies of high school graduates storm the gates to colleges and universities. Will the average youth be shut out because there is no room for those of that caliber, or will farsighted, intelligent and compassionate citizens bestir themselves to the plight of young people who may find themselves among the damned because adults have not included them in classes educated for academic survival?

Comments by Sam Lambert, Director of Research of the National Education Association in a recent NEA Journal are worth noting. He predicts "that the growth of community or junior colleges will be spurred by the desire of thousands of high school graduates to attend college. . . . Most communities of 50,000 or more will have their own junior colleges by 1970." Vocational education and specialized training are shunned by many average students. Aside from this factor, vocational training facilities are almost nonexistent in hundreds of communities and even many of those operating are outmoded and entirely inadequate for skills required today.

With recognition of the drastic shortcomings of our school systems, and, subsequently, with innovations and expansion to meet these needs, the opportunity for stimulating work in the educational field is substantial. But if we do not offer these opportunities to women, who will, as before, be carrying a large share of the responsibility of producing intelligent young men and women, much of the impact of innovation will be lost. It is more than possible that many women teachers slack off in their duties as they realize that only in rare circumstances will they have the opportunity to participate in educational activities other than classroom teaching. To embark upon a career with no notion of advancement, other than salary, particularly in this day and age when institutions are so fluid regarding personnel, is easily discouraging. There may be nothing wrong with spending thirty years in the classroom, but nowadays when people embark upon careers, they expect to move, they expect new challenges and new duties. Such expectation is crucial to the well functioning of the man on the job.

But the opportunities for women in the teaching profession to occupy positions other than in the classroom are small. The opportunities for men are greater, and consequently, men have more personal incentive to do well. It is expected, by women as well as by men, in the teaching profession that it is the men who, for the most part, will occupy the administrative and policy making positions. Even salary increments, up until a year or so ago, were higher for men than for women. Women, therefore, can rarely expect new challenges beyond the yearly turnover of classes. Of course, each new group of children presents a new challenge, but it is the rare person who doesn't see the problems and the types of personality repeating themselves. The challenge of a new job, more prestige, less familiar, and consequently, more demanding tasks, must be presented if teachers are not to be come jaded.

No one will seriously debate whether or not women are less competent than men to learn; the difficulty stems from stubborn mores, the deprecatory opinion women hold of them-

selves echoed from the attitudes of men and the past, the prevailing notion that women must look forward in large measure
to a motherhood which will not make use of their training.
"Career"—the word itself connotes a self-satisfying little venture
of safely anticipated proportions coming to a happy ending with
marriage. Even though the employment may be continued
after marriage and motherhood, the aura of personal achievement in a career seems to peter out.

Young women are improperly prepared for the multiplicity
of demands that will be made on them as workers, wives, mothers and citizens of the community. Like minorities, their talents
and potentials are inundated under the weight of specious con-
jectures. Rank discrimination still exists against women in salaries, promotion policies and job assignments. The field of politics,
for example, while seemingly as open as a book, is shot through
with "shut-out" subtleties aimed directly at the ambitious female who pictures herself in the role of a powerful politician.

Some men are unwilling to concur in the democratic
process which advocates equality of treatment and opportunity
for all. Their forces are legion, their opposition effective. The
advancement of women in unusual fields can, however, be cred-
ited to the progressive fair employment practices of government,
some businesses and industries.

While anguished warnings are heard from many sources
detailing vast shortages of trained scientists, engineers, math-
ematicians, missile technologists and other professions, women
do not enter these fields in numbers. Nor is there any dynamic
drive in force to steer them toward life work in these areas.
Students in high school and college should be encouraged to take
not only the difficult courses in mathematics and the sciences
but crash programs launched to seek and find women who have
unusual mental capacity and willingness to use their brain
power. There must be untold numbers of women who have
been lost to the United States government, research laboratories,

engineering, executive and administrative occupations, medicine and other fields. This is the effect of a reluctance on the part of both men and women to modify existing practices and institutions to meet changes we have already made toward potentialities of women.

THE MILK OF PARADISE

Agnes De Mille

Agnes De Mille is an internationally known choreographer and mother and homemaker. Her B.A., *Cum Laude,* is from the University of California. Agnes De Mille is famous for her work in such hits as "Oklahoma," "Bloomer Girl," "One Touch of Venus," "Carousel," "Allegro," "Brigadoon" and many others. She is the recipient of many awards and honorary degrees and is the author of articles and books including *Dance to the Piper* and *And Promenade Home.*

All during this separation I told myself as I wrote my husband, that when he returned I wanted to quit the theater and rest. But deep in my heart I knew I wanted nothing of the sort. Was it likely that under the stimulus and joy of his return I would suddenly bank my fires? Men have always been able to experience family and work together. It has been assumed that because of the greater emotional demands made on women, they could not have both, and they have hitherto been constrained to choose. But I was in a new century and I was greedy. I wanted wifehood, motherhood and work. I wanted all.

Two thousand years of domestic history were dead against me, and against me were the race memories and traditions I myself had inherited. But there was something else in my blood, another need, as deep and as old, and this urged without respite or peace. This would not let me be.

I had drunk the Milk of Paradise and known power. I could not think to give this up. I could forfeit my life, and my comfort,

Reprinted from *And Promenade Home* by Agnes De Mille (Boston, Atlantic Monthly Press–Little, Brown & Co., 1958). Reprinted by permission.

riches and convenience, for love—but not the magic release of
work! This was my identity.

The fact that for millennia all such desires have been ar-
bitrarily suppressed in women proves nothing but the brutality
of convention. In primitive and ancient cultures women were
thought, because they were women and because they gave birth,
to have special powers and were the preferred celebrants vital to
certain life and death occasions.

Mastery in any field is attained by practicing what is valued
at times of recognized importance. No genius, no matter what
the field, is an unprecedented accident. There must be a need,
an expectation and trust. Behind Sappho was a long line of
honored female poet-composers, the last supremely great female
composer in the history of music. She was the culmination of a
tradition[1] and it is instructive to note that Sappho was not only
by contemporary accounts (which is all we have of her, since the
music has been lost) the greatest of her profession but that she
was a good wife and mother and that her social reputation within
her community and during her lifetime was exemplary. It was a
century later that the boys in Athens started a whispering campaign of personal defamation which reinforced a growing
legend: that any woman who dedicated herself to art must be a
freak, that artistic creativity was compensation for lack of creativity in more natural and suitable functions. This myth was
not based on fact, or on any larger understanding of women's
capacities or happiness, but on men's convenience. Women have
at last, to their terrible cost, come to accept this view. It suited
their men. And they understandably wanted to suit their men.

As the conviction took hold, and woman began to think of
herself as not only different but also inferior, she gradually lost
her function as a necessary ritual voice in the community. Where
is she, for instance, in the Christian church? in the Hebraic?
the Moslem, Hindu, or Shinto? On her knees with her head

[1] There were similar priestess-musicians in Egypt, Assyria, Babylonia and
India.

covered up and her mouth shut, removed at a prophylactic dis-
tance from the high altar and all sacred vessels. In our church,
since Old Testament times, women have been considered un-
clean, a moral and ritualistic hazard. The very functions and
powers that primitive religions cherished here betray her. Since
the end of the first century A.D. women have not been allowed
to officiate in the church, build or design the church, compose
or write for the church, perform in the church,[2] nor even for
some hundreds of years sing as lay members of the congregation.
"Woman was represented [by the early Church Fathers]," writes
Lecky, "as the door of hell, as the mother of all human ills. She
should be ashamed at the very thought that she is a woman.
She should live in continual penance, on account of the curses
she had brought upon the world." [3]

Consecrated women, that is, women whose every female
function had been exorcized, neutralized and spayed, were permitted certain holy or clerical offices but always secretly, and behind bars. At one period the unsterilized were forbidden by pa-
pal edict to sing anywhere at all, even over their slop pails and
washboards. But this restriction could not long prevail. Women's
natural rejoicing while scrubbing floors and cleaning out the
garbage was not to be restrained and they gave tongue to their
enthusiasm. But only domestically. The church doors remained
shut except at a most terrible price: the dedication of her entire
life, private floorwashing and all.

And many thought the cost slight. For among other at-
tractions the church provided the only art experience the average
person, male or female, could know. During the Dark Ages its
vast projects exploited all the talent available in any community.
Throughout eight hundred years of endowed scholarship, the
church developed as many arts as it could use. But the arts it

[2] Women have been admitted to Protestant choirs only within the last
three hundred years.

[3] William Lecky, *History of European Morals, II* (New York, Braziller,
1955), pp. 357-358.

could not use—chiefly dancing—withered. No ecclesiastical or
ritual choreography was composed nor was any method of dance
notation developed, as unquestionably would have been had
the holy fathers wished to preserve any visual ceremonial. The
artists the church was permitted to use, that is, men, achieved
great works. The artists the church could not use—what became
of them? Barred up. Barred out. Wasted. Lost.

Stimulated by religious sanctions, the average husband and
father placed even harder and more cruel blocks in the path of
women's imaginative expression. By persuading themselves
and their wives that no woman could devote time to anything
but her husband and household without moral treason, they
managed to discourage undomestic yearnings. Men wanted
their wives womanly; by that was meant, we gather, that they
wanted them steadfast, attentive, enthusiastic, enduring—most
certainly enduring—and serene; and by serene was meant that
the women were to have no doubts about men's judgments and
no disturbing inclinations of their own, a concept successfully
implemented by a child a year—usually a convincer. Sixteen
children without benefit of pediatrician, nursery school or corner drugstore guaranteed attentiveness.

The women who were at the head of a great household
were in a position of considerable influence: they administered
battalions of servants; they supervised the many domestic industries which supplied virtually everything used in daily life,
and which had to be made on the premises; they ran dispensaries
for whatever medicine was needed; they arbitrated and organized and instructed. They did not, therefore, have much leisure,
and any free time was devoted to husband and children and not
to idle flights of fancy.

The women had, no doubt, great satisfaction in being necessary and effective and may well have been both serene and content; we have not heard otherwise. The important point is that
we have not heard. They were speechless. The experience of

rearing up families, which was the universal lot of all lay women, did not find in seventeen centuries a single authentic female statement.

Nor did any of the men speak up. Men have sung about acres of pearly breasts, snowy throats and bee-bruised lips, but about the service, companionship and character of his helpmeet, not one word. Until the Victorian era the sharer of bed and bosom remained "my wife, poor wretch!" Consciously or unconsciously, women have lived for hundreds, for thousands of years with the belief that their happiness lay in serving God wholly or in serving husband and children wholly. Thus by religious sanction and matrimonial reinforcement the great taboo was fixed in our mores.

For over a thousand years woman's chief creative expression was restricted to the statements of saints and visionaries locked behind walls, special in nature, in no way representative of ordinary woman, her passions or fate.

Outside the safety of the church most transgressors against the social code paid dearly for their defiance with loss of caste and cruel personal restrictions. Only lower-class women were permitted to embroider or paint, the two being considered of an equally artisan nature. Certain pretty outcasts were permitted to sing or act, although there were long periods of interdiction against even depraved women doing so. But within and without the cloister the usual price of self-expression for intellectual or wellborn women was the forfeit of sexuality.

As late as the eighteenth and nineteenth centuries, when gentlewomen began to enter what we would consider professional careers, the majority remained spinsters. The married few took husbands late when the pattern of their minds had been firmly set, like Elizabeth Barrett and George Eliot. The exception that leaps to mind is, of course, George Sand, but it must be remembered that if she had many lovers, she found by her own admission lasting happiness with no one; she remained ill-mated and lonely throughout.

And as one considers the great names of the last two centuries certain facts become apparent: many worked semi-secretly under male pseudonyms; few married, fewer still bore children; very nearly all were sick, flat on their backs as often as not.

And what kind of art did these rebellious lonely people produce? Except in two fields, not the best. There were among them a few lyric poets not comparable to the greatest men, a few second-class painters, no architect, until very recently no sculptors, not one single first-rate composer excepting the nuns Kassia, Mechtild and Hildegarde, whose work their church did not think fit to preserve but who left a tremendous contemporary reputation.

This is a fairly frightening history. It matters not a whit how you educate a girl, what techniques or attitudes you teach her. If she knows that her men will not welcome her talents she is going to proceed timidly. Put any gifted child at the keyboard, train her, exhort her six hours a day, but let it be borne in on her that in recorded music there has never been a first-rate female composer that no man will consider her work without condescension, and, worst of all, that within herself she may provide conflicts that she cannot hope to surmount, and you may get results, but they won't be Beethoven.[4]

This has been wasteful for art, cruel for the women and unhelpful to the men because they have been persuaded to build up their pride of manhood on assumptions that were bound to give way the moment women found the restraints served no good purpose and need not be endured. Today women know almost as much freedom as in pagan antiquity and turn eagerly to the arts, but to only three with promise of supreme success:

[4] It is interesting in this connection to consider what educators have found in regard to the schooling of Negro children: that they show no inferiority of endowment or application until about the eighth year when the full realization of their social status and lack of opportunity becomes clear to them. Trauma frequently cripples further development.

First, now as before, and always, to the performing careers, where in spite of long periods of interdiction and censor they have managed consistently to excel. Second, to creative story-telling and prose, in which they hold their own with the best. And third, to choreography. In this field they have practiced without restriction. No man ever barred the way here because no man thought highly enough of the business to keep women out, as he had done from so many august, holy or honorable occupations.

The Christian church had proscribed dancing and it was utterly without dignity, cut off from all serious motivation, the sources of ancient meaning and glory. The Christian church was the first great church to do this. So strongly had dancing been involved in all previous worship that it took more than one thousand years to root it out of the Catholic service (a good deal longer than it took to root women out). But it was at last eradicated and there remain now only vestigial remnants in the Mass. The church is poorer for the loss; the effect on dancing has been disastrous. For two thousand years dancing and dancers have struggled under religious and social censure more formidable than that placed on any activity, except sin itself—and sex.

Dancing nevertheless remains the germinal art, the mother of theater and all other arts, in an anthropological sense, the mother of the church. And it is in this ancient medium that those members of the community debased from proper partici-pation in more honored practices have served a quickening purpose. The rejected art and the rejected artist meet here in apt congress. Here woman is despised for her trade and not for her sex, and there is all the margin between success and failure in this differentiation. It has been the women who have trans-figured not only the art, but the point of view and purpose of its practitioners, its status and relation to other arts and to the com-munity. Dancing is the only art in which women have func-tioned to such crucial purpose, but it is the only art in which they have not worked in the teeth of universal doubt.

There have been great male choreographers—Noverre, Bournonville, Petipas, Fokine, Massine, Balanchine, Ashton, Tudor. I think one must truthfully report that the greatest have been men. But there has been no artist in a class with Michelangelo, Shakespeare, Goethe or Bach. Indeed, to rank any choreographer with these seems like impertinent hyperbole. Nor have any male figures been comparable in dynamism and originality to Isadora Duncan, Martha Graham or Mary Wigman.

The very handicaps and limitations which have frightened away gifted men work to woman's advantage. Here her training and habits stand her in good stead. Here even her body is helpful. Anonymity has been her history. She is at home in an art without literature, without past or future. She has never hoped beyond today and tomorrow—or much beyond the door of her house. Are not her daily efforts spent on evanescence? Cooking, washing, watching, caring, each day erasing the labors of the day before as each gesture erases from the air its precedent? And as every day's work must start afresh in endless repetition, so each dance begins clean, with no record. The dancer enters space without a guiding mark and the pattern is rehearsed and leaves no sign—no sign except the exchange between living people, the relationship established, if only once and never again. The patience for this is woman's special endowment. She is aware that there is no substitute for the breath of life; that it is unique and personal; that the unduplicated action, the unrepeated speech, the gesture or word thrown away or heard by few or only once may be as important as any public message. She remembers that the source is inexhaustible; that it is the moment of life that counts, the rebirth; that again and again and again the dancer jumps and runs, and when he falls, another, by vital invitation, leaps out. This, woman understands. This is the stuff of her life.

Women today comprise nearly one-third of our total working force—many thousands of them in the arts—but the ones that turn to dancing do so still for the antique reasons, power and Dionysian release on their own terms.

Dancing ranks with women's oldest professional careers, religious dedication and prostitution. It is inextricably related to both. First as priestess, then as prostitute, then as theater performer the dancer found a way of winning fortune, an excuse from household slavery and enforced seclusion.

Dancing has always produced direct fulfillment and satisfaction, and today the appeal is, as before, spellbinding through the body. It is not the concomitants of theatrical success that draw young girls so much as the vision of becoming generically *dancer* in the permitted dress, exposed legs, free and floating arms, aerial skirt. I think this is sought because it produces effects of transformation as recompense for all girls find insupportable in woman's traditional lot.

Dancing inflames and exercises the senses of the viewer (hence its long connection with prostitution) and of the performer (hence its long connection with religion). It is a physical release as no other performing art can be, because it is practiced on the whole body; the body is the instrument, the medium itself, and the exposure is total and voluptuous. Therein lies the clue to its compulsive lifelong hold. Dancing can become, more frequently than not, a substitute for physical sex, and it has all too often been chosen as a vocation because woman's sexual life in our civilization has become unsatisfactory, uncertain and expensive to the individual personality.

In what way, then, is dancing a solution? Briefly, it guarantees the satisfaction and control that people are afraid they will not gain otherwise. A dancer can do more than pray or hope; she takes matters into her own hands.

Every girl has known from time immemorial that she had better have a dowry or looks, and if she possessed neither, there was rarely any alternative for her but to become family drudge or enter the church where God could be counted on to overlook what husbands would not. Chances for a good marriage and children, for a continuing sex life, for a high income, still largely depend upon a woman's appearance. Numbers of ill-favored women have succeeded to the physical rewards of life, it is true, but it is in spite of handicap and by exercising faculties not demanded of the more handsomely endowed. Age and appearance, therefore, are important, particularly in a situation in which women outnumber men.

Doctors assure us that any feeling of inferiority induced by physical appearance, short of mutilation, is in reality a symptom of a deeper conflict, and that the truly beautiful are as capable of self-doubt as the plain. This may be so, but it is not the prevailing popular understanding.

A woman's age has always been important because her value has been reckoned chiefly as a breeding animal with fecundity determining her economic status. This is happily no longer so.

Youth and physical beauty, nevertheless, are still held up before us as a promise, and have been in legend, story and song. We are told, and we believe, women more than men, that to win love, but more imperatively, to retain love, we must be beautiful. It is a terrifying threat. And it faces us on every billboard, magazine page, screen, stage, shopwindow and, yes, even on the pages of every nursery picture book, because the princess is always beautiful or becomes so. And as we grew up, we accepted the idea more and more. Mother's friends always spoke of "the fine little boy" or "the son," but it was "the pretty little girl," and if that adjective was omitted and the word "dear" substituted, we became sensible of something hurt or slightly damaged and needing special tenderness.

Woman's best approach to happiness, we learn on all sides, is the quick rousing of men's erotic interest, and the advertisements are explicit as to what rouses men. It can be bought in a bottle—and it is quite expensive but well worth the price. Five of the largest businesses in the United States—cosmetics, ladies' clothing and accessories, furs, jewelry, both real and false, women's magazines, have sprung from the premise that romance

follows beauty and that beauty can be purchased. The young
woman is advised to make herself lovely and then lie around like
a kind of bait, and she is warned that only after the trap has
successfully sprung can she satisfy her own inclinations.

Now, for many young people this is a dismaying proposition. A girl may very well feel she cannot make the grade; she
may also feel fundamentally outraged in having her life con-
trolled by someone else's tastes, implying, as it does, a passivity
which she may interpret as helplessness.

The fact is that many women do not favor being passive,
are downright frightened by it, having witnessed centuries of
results. Young girls see quite a lot of women, particularly mothers, and often they are not enchanted. They see mothers tied to
housework who would prefer not to spend their days sweeping
and cooking. They see mothers and older sisters doing jobs and
chores which are considered more menial and less important
than fathers' jobs and that bring in no money. It is father who
has the cash for his freedom; mother must ask. Indeed, mother
has almost no freedom at all to speak of. Mothers are always at
the call of other people's needs and desires. Their daughters
find little charm in the pattern. They would like to be free to
please themselves, forever children, unless they might grow up
to some of the freedom of father. But growing up for a woman,
as they observe, seems to mean less freedom, and no guarantee of
happiness. And so some of them, the dancers, never grow up.

Very few dancers develop the bodies of mature women;
they keep lean in the hips and flat-breasted, a phenomenon re-
marked by all costume designers. It is also a fact that the greatest
performers, the women best capable of communicating sensuous
satisfaction, are in their bodies least sensual. In effect they have
sacrificed all organs of personal fulfullment and maintain and
cherish only the means for public satisfaction, the system of
bones and sinews for levitation and propulsion. The ballet foot
and leg, when used to its full capacity, can evoke an almost
physical response; in repose it is as tight and straight as the

leg of a mule. Certain great soloists have been lacking in even primary sexual functions and are known to have menstruated rarely. For the rest, very many, possibly a majority, are partially frigid and most tend to be, in spite of legend, more chaste than otherwise. I do not mean to imply that they are not passionate and gallant, but that certain deep rejections and fears prevent easy sexual release. The majority of American women are, it is claimed by medical statistics, partially frigid, and perhaps dancers no more than others. In any case, the dancers have evolved a substitute expression and do not mind the state so bitterly. This, of course, is no good answer to the fear of life. But it is an instinctive and practical one.

Even Isadora Duncan, who clamored the loudest for love, was no exception. She was a true sensualist and she seems to belie in the richness of her experience all I have argued about the dance as a substitute for life. But consider her point of view repeatedly expressed: she avowed when very young never to submit to woman's usual fate; never to marry, that is, never to put herself or her fortune into any man's keeping; to bear children if and when she pleased; to leave them or look after them at whim; to be absolutely free and to remain so. She wished to have the freedom of a pagan as she imagined it, for she recognized love as a transient ecstasy. The communion on which marriage is built she never, I believe, envisaged, nor constancy, security, fruition, these being the rewards of the female life she scorned. She followed a dream, power without responsibility, release without cost. And her way of attainment was the cultivation of her body. The littlest ballet pupil in first position before the mirror is starting on the same historic path.[5]

For in dancing the face matters least and the body is beautiful if it functions beautifully. It is not the shape of the leg, but the use of the leg that tells. Furthermore, and most felicitously,

---

[5] I would like to interject that very few daughters of contented mothers have become ballerinas. I cannot name a father who urged a dancing career on his girl unless he was himself a dancer and looked upon the matter as one of natural succession.

the beautiful use changes the flesh and corrects all manner of
imperfections. Contrary to maxims, by taking thought one can
add a cubit to stature. When a dancer stands before a mirror,
she no longer sees what her big brothers see, but a promise. If
her nose turns up or down, no matter: men will gasp at the car-
riage of her head. If she is fat, she will get thin. If she is thin, the
muscles of her back and thighs will enable her to move like a
voluptuary. And who is to say or who cares what she is, whether
this or that, if she stands in the center of a stage in the revealing
and beautiful uniform of her trade, escorted by the best cavalier
in the business, who has forfeited the right to refuse her and
must take her if she is the best, not the prettiest, mind you, but
the best and the most skillful. And there, for all to see, in public,
she will perform with him the ritual of romantic courtship. In
no other art are the rewards as enormous, the attention as
direct, admiration as spontaneous, emotional release as full. The
audience remains always under the performer's command. She
never surrenders her will. Her rewards are taken directly by her
own effort. No intermediary is needed—and for any female who
doubts her powers this is a temptation of frightening persuasive-
ness.

Dancing represents sex in its least costly form, free from
imprisonment and free to a great extent from emotional responsibility, and, above all, as a sure thing, independent of someone
else's pleasure. In other words, it means freedom from sex. The
forces which impelled women to the austerity of the church
operate to form the great dancer. In a strange transmutation
dancing is a form of asceticism—almost a form of celibacy.

Is, then, the aesthetic impulse rooted in neurosis and unable to develop except under the compulsion of pain? Are these
brutal disciplines and forfeits necessary to creative effort? The
ancients did not rely on any such goads and, notwithstanding,
their art flourished. The restraints we place on women creators
could well be accidental to our culture, of no great profit to the
individual or the work, but, rather, destructive to both. I believe

this to be the case; the genius with which certain women write or paint or compose or choreograph derives from faculties and needs beyond any mere act of compensation. Talent is compounded of the entire personality and is as much a sign of exuberant health as of sickness. But the bewitchment of hundreds of thousands, of millions of girls by the dream, by even the discipline of dancing, cannot be called creativity, nor even vocation. It is escape, it is protest, and it is, in large part, hysterical protest.

For a time such a purpose serves the art form well, but only for a time. In the working conditions of our world and theater the dedicated performers are forced under emotional whips to greater and greater effort. But there is a limit. The personality ceases to expand, ceases to breathe; in certain aspects it withers, and this is reflected in a stunting of the art. The audience is always aware. An act of suppression that cancels out emotional or imaginative life, one at the cost of the other, is obviously wasteful. With either choice a major section of the personality is wrecked and all human relations, in marriage and out, must suffer.

A dancer's release, like most magic, is transient and won each time by renewed and arduous effort. Dancing has become, consequently, a kind of sexual limbo whose inhabitants identify their own flesh with their purpose, a confusion not equally true for women artists whose bodies are not their life work. Dancing is, in a deep sense, the only physical union many of these women know, a sort of automarriage. And as with all such narcissistic unions, there develops an aura of melancholy and the promise of death. Many a young dancer has drowned in the mirrors before which she spends her life. The others live only when the reflection from the audience fans breath back into their emptying spirits.

Whatever rewards the dancer knows in place of the usual emotional and sexual associations, she is frequently assailed by doubts in her late twenties or early thirties. Even the very great know these morbid spells. The needs of the heart cannot be cheated forever. The dancer grows frightened. She realizes suddenly she is a spinster and aging, no matter how fast she gets around the room. The life of merciless effort, the dimming chances of permanent fame, exhaustion and a growing comprehension of what old age means to a fading athlete without family or home suddenly terrify even the stanchest. The sacrifice, perhaps, has been too much, and perhaps not necessary. There is many a volte-face at this point and a marriage with at least one child in a frantic effort to put life back on balance.

But our theater is not set up for family life; dancing in particular is conditioned by world-wide touring, uncertain and irregular seasons, precarious pay. Dancers today do not inherit the career dynastically as they used to, like the Vestris, the Taglioni (five distinguished members, and three generations in this family), the Grisi, Elssler, Karsavin clans. Our dancers are not protected wards of state with guaranteed salaries and pensions. The married dancer is called upon to relinquish jobs that would further her career and settle for domesticity against professional interest. Many do this serenely and good-naturedly; this is nothing more than the problem of reconciling life and art, which is present with all workers, but in a dancer's case, particularly for women, it is final. She may consider the exchange worth the price either way. She may not, and live in perpetual conflict.

It is astonishing under the circumstances that none of these factors deters young girls one whit. Five million of them in this country alone are studying to be professional dancers. Perhaps this is so because women today, even dancers, cannot bring themselves to accept these conditions as permanent. They see no reason why they should not have both work and family, what with Deepfreeze, Waring blenders and diaper service. They believe also with all their hearts and hopes—because it suits them so to believe—that sweet reasonableness and a sense of fair play will dissolve the major block to the double life: their husbands' attitude.

Marriage is difficult with any artist. "A man does not love a woman for her genius; he loves her in spite of her genius," writes Maurice Goudeket, the husband of Colette. Marriage is perhaps hardest of all with a theater personality because the work is not wholly under the control of the individual. Dancers, above all, do not make easy wives. The union has to run a gamut of conflicting loyalties. A dancer's husband has to share his wife's discipline. His life is as curtailed as hers and quite literally by hers. Most men, particularly men outside of the profession, find such conditions onerous.

But the unrest is general and pertains to all careers and all classes of society. Preachers, doctors and teachers warn; magazine and newspaper editorialize. The women's magazines are particularly explicit: if the wife has to work outside the home she must never let it impinge on her husband's schedule, and if inside the home she must see that it is finished and put away before he comes back from his own work and she must never for one moment let him think that hers is more important than his, or his interests and hobbies and needs. And for this reason, and because it will be construed as a direct reflection on his virility, she must not earn more money. He will develop ulcers, sinuses, abscesses, tuberculosis. He will borrow the classic symptom of women's frustration, the bitter, black headache, and although women's magazines do not care to name this, he will add one of his own, partial or total impotence, which is a form of suicide and just as unanswerable. He may in the end leave her.

If the women do not depend on their men as their grandmothers did, the men similarly manage to do without them. It has become a game of mutual attrition played out on a level on which both are pitifully defenseless. Medical statistics and divorce courts list the ruin. The suicide rate among men, the alcoholism, the excesses of sedation and narcotics, the growing overt homosexuality, the juvenile neuroticism and delinquency attest to the monumental cost of the emotional adjustment. This is the "furious and lamentable region" that Conrad speaks of, "the dwelling place of unveiled hearts" where there is neither right nor wrong but only human suffering.

Woman has always accepted with grace, with pride and satisfaction, her husband's interests and achievements, taking joy, without any sense of diminution and shame. Can the husband endure to learn this? Does he wish to? Will he not rather attempt to put things back as they were, stuffing all hopes, ambitions and zests not centered on himself into the family cupboard and setting his back to the door? Indeed, indeed, things cannot go back. Pandora's box is opened. The girls are earning money.

It is of no consequence who works better, men or women; it is important that each work differently and that each be allowed to try without penalties. "Never destroy any aspect of personality," said my Grandmother George, who had no career except caring for her family, "for what you think is the wild branch may be the heart of the tree." Not all women want a double life. But those who do should not be denied on the grounds of sex. It is not easy to be a devoted wife and mother and a first-class artist; it is equally hard to be an artist with no root experience in life. It is impossible to be a good wife or a wise mother, embittered, balked and devoured by inner energies. Creative exercise can be disciplined to a household schedule—not easily, but women everywhere prove it can be done. For when all faculties are exercised the enormous releases of strength and satisfaction more than make up for the extra attention demanded. Extra attention? No, rather, elimination of waste and repining. The alternation of diaper washing and composing spell one another in mutual refreshment. Ask any responsible working mother. And the children will reflect the zest and energy of the parent's life—and as to the work, how it flourishes! How it flowers and expands! Even under discipline, perhaps particularly under discipline, because it is voluntary and joyful, because the sources of life are fulfilled and replenished and because, as in all things, the greater the range of accomplishment, the greater the capacity for more.

I think this is what Isadora Duncan meant when she spoke of founding a new religion: the total release of women's hearts, the total use of their gifts.

Women have bent to the yoke and the scars of their durance are upon their children. But with the lessening of all social and religious restrictions, with widening economic opportunities, with practical invention bringing ease and leisure, there stands between woman and whatever life she yearns for one important barrier: her husband's good will. Failing this, she fails all. She must have his blessing, his pride in her achievement. Let him dower her with this and the great works for which we have waited so long will come. But beyond and beneath, comes happiness.

It is an act of recognition that is needed, an act of love.